A USER'S GUIDE TO THE JCT ARBITRATION RULES

A USER'S GUIDE TO THE JCT ARBITRATION RULES

Neil F. Jones

LLB(Hons), ACIArb,
Solicitor of the Supreme Court

BSP PROFESSIONAL BOOKS

OXFORD LONDON EDINBURGH

BOSTON MELBOURNE

First published 1989

British Library
Cataloguing in Publication Data
Jones, Neil F.
  A user's guide to the JCT arbitration
rules.
  1. Great Britain. Buildings. Construction.
Contracts. Disputes. Arbitration
  I. Title
  692.8'0941

ISBN 0–632–02496–8

BSP Professional Books
A division of Blackwell Scientific
  Publications Ltd
Editorial Offices:
Osney Mead, Oxford OX2 0EL
  (Orders: Tel. 0865 240201)
8 John Street, London WC1N 2ES
23 Ainslie Place, Edinburgh EH3 6AJ
3 Cambridge Center, Suite 208, Cambridge,
  MA 02142, USA
107 Barry Street, Carlton, Victoria 3053,
  Australia

Set by DMD, St Clements Oxford
Printed and bound in Great Britain by
Mackays of Chatham PLC, Chatham, Kent

To Mary, Claire and Mandy.

Contents

Preface

Arbitration in the building industry is commonplace. Many disputes and differences which are referred to arbitration arise out of the use of the standard forms of contract produced by the Joint Contracts Tribunal for the Standard Form of Building Contract. The production by such a body of Arbitration Rules is therefore of considerable importance for all those engaged in such arbitrations.

This book is intended as a guide to these new Rules for those who will be making use of them. This will include arbitrators, lawyers, lay advocates and parties representing themselves. It is not intended as a book on the law or practice of arbitration generally. There are ample learned works to which those interested can refer. The citing of cases has been kept to an absolute minimum. However frequent reference has been made to sections of the Arbitration Act 1950 ('The 1950 Act') and the Arbitration Act 1979 ('The 1979 Act') as knowledge of these two statutes is essential background if the Rules are to be understood and operated properly in practice.

I have chosen to restrict my comments generally to domestic arbitrations which I have treated as being those arbitrations subject to the law of England and Wales and where the parties are either individuals who are nationals or are habitually resident in the United Kingdom or are bodies corporate incorporated in, or whose central management or control is exercised in, the United Kingdom. Having said this, this Guide is nevertheless equally applicable even where there is a foreign element if the agreement to arbitrate contains a provision incorporating the 1950 Act (notwithstanding section 34 thereof) and the 1979 Act – see for example clause 41.7 of JCT 80; clause 38.8 of NSC/4; clause 10.6 of NSC/2; clause 9.7 of the JCT Management Contract; clause 9.7 of Works Contract/2 and clause 7.6 of Works Contract/3.

The Arbitration Rules are not applicable to Scottish building contracts. However, there is no reason in principle why they should not be used, subject to allowances being made for differences in the respective systems of law.

Many people have helped me directly or indirectly in connection with the preparation of this book. They are too numerous to mention individually but I thank them all. However, I must specifically mention firstly Julia Burden, Commissioning Editor for the Publishers of this book for her great patience and fine sense of judgment in granting me numerous extensions of time for delivery of the script. Secondly, I must mention Mary, my wife who has suffered the double indignity of seeing me locked away in the study during what should otherwise be social hours and then being asked to enter the text onto a word processor disk.

Finally, I join with the Publishers in gratefully acknowledging the kind permission of RIBA Publications Limited to include a copy of the Rules in Appendix 4 to this book.

February 1989
NEIL F. JONES
Neil F. Jones & Co.
Royton House
George Road
Edgbaston
Birmingham B15 1NU

Chapter 1

Background to the JCT Arbitration Rules

Introduction

On 18 July 1988 the Joint Contracts Tribunal for the Standard Form of Building Contract published for the first time a set of arbitration rules. In JCT terms this may be said to have been a happy occasion as the desire to see these arbitration rules published to assist the conduct of construction industry arbitrations under JCT contracts was fully supported by all the constituent bodies of the Tribunal, representing private and public employers, contractors, sub-contractors and the construction industry professions. The reason for such wholehearted support can undoubtedly be attributed to the impression, widely held by users of the arbitration process in the construction industry, that it is often far too slow and expensive.

The Chairman of the Tribunal at the date of publication, Patrick Barry, said when launching the JCT Arbitration Rules:

'As you know, the JCT proceeds by consensus among its constituent bodies and on occasions that consensus is not easy to reach. However, perhaps uniquely in our fifty odd years of work, the documents before you today have from the beginning received wide support.

Indeed, the main concern of constituent bodies has been an anxiety to reach publication as early as possible.'

The purpose of the Rules

The JCT Arbitration Rules seek to reduce or eliminate unnecessary delays and expense. It is important to stress that it is the *unnecessary* delays and costs which the Rules, properly used, will help to reduce or eliminate. They are not an attempt to save time and money by eating into the fundamental principles of natural justice and fairness. Where, in order for a party to properly present its case, it is necessary to take a certain amount of time and incur certain sums in costs then this is accommodated within the Rules.

To attempt to use the Rules oppressively so as to prevent a party from adequately presenting its case would amount to a serious misuse of the Rules. Throughout the remainder of this book when discussing the Rules, reference will be made time and again to the need to follow the principles of natural justice and no apology is made for this. By natural justice is meant the duty on the part of the arbitrator to act fairly and to be *seen* to be acting fairly to all parties to the arbitration. In more specific terms it includes the following:

- the arbitrator must be disinterested, unbiased and impartial;
- each party must be given a fair opportunity to present its case, to know the case it has to meet and to meet the opposing case. It may be that unless custom or practice or specific rules governing the arbitration provide otherwise (as do the JCT Arbitration Rules in appropriate circumstances), the right to present one's own case and to meet the opponent's case includes a right to have an oral hearing where witnesses can be examined and cross-examined.

Provided these fundamental principles of fairness are followed, a positive and robust use of the Rules by the arbitrator will, as will be seen, enable him to keep a very tight control over the manner in which the proceedings are conducted and the timescale within which they operate.

Lord Justice Donaldson (as he then was) in the case of *F.G. Whitley and Sons* v. *Clwyd County Council* (1982) put the matter this way:

'It is for arbitrators to decide how the arbitration shall be conducted. In doing so, it is of the very greatest importance that they shall keep control of the proceedings. Having given due consideration to any arguments which may be addressed to them, they should make firm decisions, leaving it to the parties to take such action, whether by appeal or otherwise, as may be open to them. No arbitrator should be criticised for taking a wrong decision, provided that it is not unfair or contrary to the rules of natural justice, but he will indeed be open to criticism if he is not firm.'

This question of fairness and evenhandedness is discussed further when dealing with the arbitrator's powers – see page 70 – and when considering the choice of procedure for the conduct of the arbitration – see page 85.

Clearly, if the arbitrator and the parties are competent, experienced and co-operative, then even without rules governing the conduct of the arbitration, there is likely to be little waste of time or costs. The test of the ability in practice of the JCT Arbitration Rules to control time and cost will be judged in relation to arbitrations where one of the parties is reluctant to proceed regularly and diligently with the process. The Rules contain a number of strict time limits to deal with this situation and even, though to a more limited extent, where all parties to the arbitration are guilty of procrastination.

However zealous the arbitrator may be in seeking to ensure that time-tables are adhered to and that one party does not abuse the process of arbitration in order to create delay or confusion, the arbitrator must always remain impartial and detached. If he forms, on reasonable grounds, the view that one party is deliberately delaying matters, or is unreasonably delaying them, the arbitrator's remedy is to use the powers at his disposal under any applicable arbitration rules or through the courts. He should refrain from taking sides in such a situation. As was said in the case of *Turner (East Asia) Pte Ltd* v. *Builders Federal (Hong Kong) Ltd and Josef Gartner & Co.* (1988) (Singapore) by Judicial Commissioner Chao Hick Tin:

> 'There can be no doubt that an arbitrator must always act judicially with a detached mind and with patience. He must not at any time descend into the arena or take an adversarial role. His response and words used must always be measured and circumspect.'

On no account should the arbitrator enter the fray between the parties.

The role of the lawyer

Lawyers have an important role to play in arbitration. This does not mean that they ought to be involved in every arbitration or that their involvement must always follow a rigid pattern. Some arbitrations do not require lawyers for the dispute be satisfactorily resolved. Others require a contribution from a lawyer which is less than a full service of advice, pleadings, case preparation and representation at the hearing. Sometimes the only contribution need be some general advice. On other occasions it will be appropriate for a lawyer to draft a statement of case or a statement of defence and on other occasions to appear at a hearing to deal with an identified legal issue whilst not taking part in relation to purely technical matters. The key is to know when faced with a dispute, exactly what sort of contribution is required. This may mean that a lawyer should be consulted in the majority of cases. It is then for the lawyer to gain a full (and rapid) appreciation of the issues involved so that informed decisions can be taken.

It is undoubtedly the case that, if parties are not legally represented when they ought to have been, the result can be chaotic, time consuming and expensive. A good example of this occurred in the case of *C.M.A. Maltin Engineering Limited* v. *J. Donne Holdings Limited* (1980) where the arbitrator departed from the rules of natural justice but the unrepresented parties did not fully appreciate the position. In this case, Mr Justice Bingham made some pertinent remarks. He said firstly that:

> '. . . a party who seeks, for understandable reasons, to dispense with the formalities of ordinary litigation should not without more be treated as wishing to dispense with the fundamental rules underlying the administration of all justice, however informal; and while the court should be slow to intermeddle with the procedural conduct of arbitrations, it has a responsibility to safeguard the ultimate integrity of the arbitration process.'

Later on when holding that one of the parties had not waived a departure by the arbitrator from the principles of natural justice; namely receiving a document from one party and refusing to show it or a copy of it to the other party, the same judge said as follows:

> 'Donne were appearing, without legal assistance or advice, before a legally qualified arbitrator. In these circumstances it would be natural for the party to rely on the expertise and experience of the arbitrator to safeguard his interests where the observance of cardinal procedural rules was concerned, even (perhaps particularly) within the framework of an informal arbitration. It would, I think, be unsatisfactory if uninformed

reliance on the correctness of an arbitrator's ruling were held to debar a party from seeking relief on learning that a serious error had been committed.'

Where a party is not legally represented, more particularly where the arbitration process is an informal one, the arbitrator has to be scrupulously fair. If he himself is inexperienced or incompetent, the result is likely to be disastrous. See for example the case of *Pratt* v. *Swanmore Builders Limited and Baker* (1980).

Despite these cautionary words, arbitrators must be prepared to be bold and firm. Fear of making a wrong decision, while understandable and possibly beneficial if it leads to increased care and consideration being taken in forming a view, must not be allowed to lead to a failure to make any firm decision at all. To err is human.

As will be seen, the JCT Arbitration Rules provide a choice of procedures ranging from a short expedited oral hearing with very little documentation, through a documents only procedure, to a full procedure with an oral hearing in many respects similar (though in some important respects different) from those which typically take place at the present time in relation to large complicated construction disputes.

Chapter 2

Scope and application of the JCT Arbitration Rules

Introduction

The use of the JCT Arbitration Rules is prescribed in all JCT contracts, sub-contracts and other agreements. The reference to the Rules in these contracts is contained in what are called the Arbitration Agreements – see Rule 1. The table below identifies the title of the contract in the left-hand column, the article/clause number containing the Arbitration Agreement in the centre column and the JCT contract amendment number which introduces the Rules in the right-hand column.

Contract	Article or clause Reference	JCT amendment no
(1) The Standard Form of Building Contract 1980 Edition, as amended, all versions	Article 5 and clause 41	Amendment 6
(2) The Standard Forms of Employer/ Nominated Sub-Contractor Agreement (NSC/2 and NSC/2a), 1980 Edition, as amended	Clause 10 (NSC/2) Clause 8 (NSC/2a)	Amendment 2
(3) The JCT Standard Forms of Nominated Sub-Contract NSC/4 and NSC/4a, 1980 Edition, as amended	Article 3 and clause 38	Amendment 6
(4) The JCT Warranty by a Nominated Supplier (TNS/2: Schedule 3 of the JCT Standard Form of Tender by Nominated Supplier), as amended	Clause 4	Amendment 1
(5) The Standard Form of Building Contract with Contractor's Design 1981 Edition, as amended	Article 5 and clause 39	Amendment 4
(6) The Intermediate Form of Building Contract for Works of simple content 1984 Edition, as amended	Article 5 and section 9	Amendment 3

Contract	Article or clause Reference	JCT amendment no
(7) The Standard Form of Sub-Contract Conditions for Sub-Contractors named under the Intermediate Form of Building Contract (NAM/SC), 1984 Edition, as amended	Article 4 and clause 35	Amendment 3
(8) The Standard Form of Management Contract 1987 Edition, as amended	Article 8 and section 9	Amendment 1
(9) The Standard Form of Works Contract (Works Contract/1 and Works Contract/2) 1987 Edition for use with the Standard Form of Management Contract, as amended	Works Contract/1, Section 3 Article 3 and Works Contract/2 section 9	Amendment 1
(10) The Standard Form of Employer/ Works Contractor Agreement (Works Contract/3*) 1987 Edition, as amended	Clause 7	Amendment 1
(11) The Agreement for Minor Building Works 1980 Edition, as amended	Article 4 and clause 9	Amendment MW5

* (Note – the Rules refer to Works Contract/1 which must be a printing error.)

There are certain related forms of contract published by the Building Employers Confederation including the domestic sub-contracts for use with JCT 80 Standard Form of Building Contract, the JCT Standard Form of Building Contract With Contractor's Design, the JCT Intermediate Form of Building Contract (IFC 84) and also the form of direct agreement between Employer and Named Sub-Contractor for use with the Intermediate Form, namely Form ESA/1. It can be anticipated that these forms of contract will be amended to incorporate the Rules.

The precise wording of the Arbitration Agreements in the different contracts varies. In particular the Arbitration Agreements to be found in the JCT Agreement for Minor Building Works, NSC/2 and NSC/2a, and TNS/2 are less detailed.

Commentary on Arbitration Agreements

For the purpose of commentary one of the fuller Arbitration Agreements has been selected, namely, that which appears in the Standard Form of Building Contract JCT 80 in all its versions.

Article 5 of JCT 80 provides:

Article 5

'If any dispute or difference as to the construction of this contract [sic Contract] or any matter or thing of whatsoever nature arising thereunder or in connection therewith shall arise between the Employer or the Architect on his behalf and the Contractor either during the progress or after the completion or abandonment of the Works, except under clause 31 (statutory tax deduction scheme) to the extent provided on [sic in] clause 31.9 or under clause 3 of the VAT Agreement, it shall be and is hereby referred to arbitration in accordance with clause 41.'

As can be seen, provision is made that any dispute or difference as to the construction of the contract or any matter or thing of whatsoever nature arising thereunder or in connection therewith shall be and is thereby referred to arbitration in accordance with clause 41. The phrase '. . . arising thereunder or in connection therewith . . .' which appeared also in clause 35 of JCT 63, has been given a liberal interpretation by the Court of Appeal in the case of *Ashville Investments Limited* v. *Elmer Contractors Limited* (1987) so as to bestow upon the arbitrator a jurisdiction which includes the power to grant rectification of the contract arising out of alleged innocent or negligent misrepresentation. Despite this liberal interpretation, Amendment 6 to JCT 80, along with the amendments to the Arbitration Agreements in the other JCT contracts listed earlier, with the exception of the direct employer/ sub-contractor, works contractor or supplier agreements (NSC/2 and NSC/2a, Works Contract/3 and TNS/1) expressly give the arbitrator power to rectify the contract so that it accurately reflects the true agreement made by the employer and contractor or contractor and sub-contractor or works contractor, as the case may be.

Clause 41 of JCT 80 in all its versions following Amendment 6 now provides as follows:

41.1   When the Employer or the Contractor require a dispute or difference as referred to in Article 5 including:

> any matter or thing left by this Contract to the discretion of the Architect, or

> the withholding by the Architect of any certificate to which the Contractor may claim to be entitled, or

> the adjustment of the Contract Sum under clause 30.6.2, or

the rights and liabilities of the parties under clauses 27, 28, 32 or 33, or

unreasonable withholding of consent or agreement by the Employer or the Architect on his behalf or by the Contractor

to be referred to arbitration then either the Employer or the Contractor shall give written notice to the other to such effect and such dispute or difference shall be referred to the arbitration and final decision of a person to be agreed between the parties as the Arbitrator, or, upon failure so to agree with 14 days after the date of the aforesaid written notice, of a person to be appointed as the Arbitrator on the request of either the Employer or the Contractor by the person named in the Appendix.

41.2 .1 Provided that if the dispute or difference to be referred to arbitration under this Contract raises issues which are substantially the same as or connected with issues raised in a related dispute between:

the Employer and Nominated Sub-Contractor under Agreement NSC/2 or NSC/2a as applicable, or

the Contractor and any Nominated Sub-Contractor under Sub-contract NSC/4 or NSC/4a as applicable, or

the Contractor and/or the Employer and any Nominated Supplier whose contract of sale with the Contractor provides for the matters referred to in clause 36.4.8.2,

and if the related dispute has already been referred for determination to an Arbitrator, the Employer and the Contractor hereby agree

that the dispute or difference under this Contract shall be referred to the Arbitrator appointed to determine the related dispute;

that the JCT Arbitration Rules applicable to the related dispute shall apply to the dispute under this Contract;

that such Arbitrator shall have power to make such directions and all necessary awards in the same way as if the procedure of the High Court as to joining one or more defendants or joining co-defendants or third parties was available to the parties and to him; and that the agreement and consent referred to in clause 41.6 on appeals or applications to the High Court on any question of law shall apply to any question of law arising out of the awards of such Arbitrator in respect of all related disputes referred to him or arising in the course of the reference of all the related disputes referred to him;

41.2 .2 save that the Employer or the Contractor may require the dispute or difference under this Contract to be referred to a different Arbitrator (to be appointed under this Contract) if either of them reasonably considers that the Arbitrator appointed to determine the related dispute is not appropriately qualified to determine the dispute or difference under this Contract.

41.2 .3 Clauses 41.2.1 to 41.2.2 shall apply unless in the Appendix the words 'clauses 41.2.1 and 41.2.2 apply' have been deleted.

41.3 Such reference, except

　　.1 on article 3 or article 4; or

　　.2 on the questions
　　　　whether or not the issue of an instruction is empowered by the Conditions; or
　　　　whether or not a certificate has been improperly withheld; or
　　　　whether a certificate is not in accordance with the Conditions; or
　　　　whether a determination under clause 22C.4.3.1 will be just and equitable; or

　　.3 on any dispute or difference under clause 4.1 in regard to a reasonable objection by the Contractor, under clause 8.4, under clause 18.1 or clause 23.3.2 in regard to withholding of consent by the Contractor, and clauses 25, 32 and 33,

shall not be opened until after Practical Completion or alleged Practical Completion of the Works or termination or alleged termination of the Contractor's employment under this Contract or abandonment of the Works, unless with the written consent of the Employer or the Architect on his behalf and the Contractor.

41.4 Subject to the provisions of clauses 4.2, 30.9, 38.4.3, 39.5.3 and 40.5 the Arbitrator shall, without prejudice to the generality of his powers, have power to rectify the contract so that it accurately reflects the true agreement made by the Employer and the Contractor, to direct such measurements and/or valuations as may in his opinion be desirable in order to determine the rights of the parties and to ascertain and award any sum which ought to have been the subject of or included in any certificate and to open up, review and revise any certificate, opinion, decision (except, where clause 8.4. is relevant, a decision of the Architect to issue instructions pursuant to clause 8.4.1), requirement or notice and to determine all matters in dispute which shall be submitted to him in the same manner as if no such certificate, opinion, decision, requirement or notice had been given.

41.5 Subject to clause 41.6 the award of such Arbitrator shall be final and binding on the parties.

41.6 The parties hereby agree and consent pursuant to Sections 1(3)(a) and 2(1)(b) of the Arbitration Act, 1979, that either party

.1 may appeal to the High Court on any question of law arising out of an award made in an arbitration under this Arbitration Agreement; and

.2 may apply to the High Court to determine any question of law arising in the course of the reference;

and the parties agree that the High Court should have jurisdiction to determine any such question of law.

41.7 Whatever the nationality, residence or domicile of the Employer, the Contractor, any sub-contractor or supplier or the Arbitrator, and wherever the Works or any part thereof are situated, the law of England shall be the proper law of this Contract and in particular (but not so as to derogate from the generality of the foregoing) the provisions of the Arbitration Acts 1950 (notwithstanding anything in section 34 thereof) to 1979 shall apply to any arbitration under this Contract wherever the same, or any part of it, shall be conducted. [y.2]

41.8 If before making his final award the Arbitrator dies or otherwise ceases to act as the Arbitrator, the Employer and the Contractor shall forthwith appoint a further Arbitrator, or, upon failure so to appoint within 14 days of any such death or cessation, then either the Employer or the Contractor may request the person named in the Appendix to appoint such further Arbitrator. Provided that no such further Arbitrator shall be entitled to disregard any direction of the previous Arbitrator or to vary or revise any award of the previous Arbitrator except to the extent that the previous Arbitrator had power so to do under the JCT Arbitration Rules and/or with the agreement of the parties and/or by the operation of law.

41.9   The arbitration shall be conducted in accordance with the 'JCT Arbitration Rules' current at the Base Date. [y.3]. Provided that if any amendments to the Rules so current have been issued by the Joint Contracts Tribunal after the Base Date the Employer and the Contractor may, by a joint notice in writing to the Arbitrator, state that they wish the arbitration to be conducted in accordance with the JCT Arbitration Rules as so amended.

Footnote
[y.2] Where the parties do not wish the proper law of the Contract to be the law of England appropriate amendments to clause 41.7 should be made. Where the Works are situated in Scotland then the forms issued by the Scottish Building Committee which contain Scots proper law and arbitration provisions are the appropriate documents. It should be noted that the provisions of the Arbitration Acts 1950 to 1979 do not extend to Scotland.

[y.3] The JCT Arbitration Rules contain stricter time limits than those prescribed by some arbitration rules or those frequently observed in practice. The parties should note that a failure by a party or the agent of a party to comply with the time limits incorporated in these Rules may have adverse consequences.

(1) Scope of disputes or differences referable to arbitration

Two types of dispute or difference are excluded from the Arbitration Agreement, namely:

● those concerning the Statutory Tax Deduction Scheme under the Finance (No 2) Act 1975 and the Income Tax (Sub-Contractors in the Construction Industry) Regulations 1975 SI No 1960 to the extent that the Act or Regulations or any other Act of Parliament or Statutory Instrument rule or order provides for some other method of resolving such dispute or difference.

● those concerning any employer's challenge in regard to Value Added Tax claimed by the contractor in which case the matter is dealt with in accordance with clause 3 of the Supplemental Provisions (the VAT Agreement) incorporated into JCT 80 by virtue of clause 15.1 of the Conditions.

Clause 41.1 includes a number of specific types of dispute or difference which the employer or contractor may require to be referred to arbitration. They are in themselves very wide, but even so they do not detract from the general scope of the wording in Article 5 '. . . any dispute or difference as to the construction of this contract [sic Contract] or any matter or thing of whatsoever nature arising thereunder or in connection therewith . . .'. (See page 8.) The specific matters referred to in clause 41.1 include any matters left by the contract to the discretion of the architect, the withholding by the architect of a certificate; adjustments of the contract sum; rights and liabilities upon determination and the withholding of consent or agreement by the employer or the architect or by the contractor.

(2) *The notice and commencement of the arbitration*

It is now made clearer by clause 41.1 that one party must give to the other a written notice requiring the dispute or difference to be referred to arbitration (already in NSC/4 or NSC/4a). This express provision is useful even though the need for a written notice was in any event clearly apparent from other words in the Arbitration Agreements, for example, the words in clause 41.1 of JCT 80 prior to Amendment 6, '. . . failing agreement within 14 days after either party has given to the other a written request to concur in the appointment of an Arbitrator . . .'.

In the case of *Emson Contractors Limited* v. *Protea Estates Limited* (1987) the court considered the Arbitration Agreement in an earlier version of JCT 80 together with the reference in clause 30.9.3 to the words 'If any arbitration or other proceedings have been commenced . . .'. This particular wording remains unchanged. His Honour Judge Fox-Andrews Q.C. was of the view, not having however heard argument on the point from counsel, that *commenced* meant that one party had invited the other to agree to a named person as arbitrator, or, where one party made a written request to the other to concur in the appointment of an arbitrator, whichever first occurred. The issue is now probably put beyond doubt. The arbitration commences for the purposes of clause 30.9 and for limitation purposes under the Limitation Act 1980 section 34(3) when one party gives written notice as is now expressly required under clause 41.1. One slight doubt remains as a result of the continued use of the phrase, e.g. in Article 5 that any dispute or difference which arises '. . . shall be *and is hereby* referred to arbitration . . .' whereby it might be argued, somewhat faintly, that the arbitration has commenced automatically upon a dispute or difference arising. The obvious inconvenience of such a construction would tend against its being accepted.

As arbitration depends upon an agreement to arbitrate between the parties and also because the notice referring the dispute or difference to arbitration will generally stop time from running for limitation purposes, it is important that the notice describes the dispute or difference in the broadest possible terms, otherwise the recipient of the notice may argue at a later date that a claim actually being made in the arbitration as identified in the statement of case is outside the scope of the written notice. Indeed, the objecting party may even be able to set aside the arbitrator's award made on matters outside the scope of the written notice where that party has properly reserved its position as to the arbitrator's lack of authority, despite having gone ahead with the arbitration, including the claim objected to. Some specimen notices to refer disputes or differences to arbitration opt for the broadest possible wording such as 'I require you to concur with me in the appointment of an arbitrator for the settlement of the disputes which have arisen between us . . .' (see *Russell on Arbitration* 20th Edition published by Stephens & Sons).

While this may be the safest course it may not be the most helpful. A possible answer is to be as specific as possible in defining the disputes or differences which have arisen and to conclude with some such phrase as 'without prejudice to the particularity of the foregoing any other disputes or differences which have arisen between us'.

(3) Agreeing the arbitrator

Clause 41.1 requires the dispute or difference to be referred to a person to be agreed between the parties. If no agreement is reached within 14 days of the written notice, either party can request an appointment to be made by the president or a vice president of whichever appointing body has been selected in the appendix to the contract, namely the Royal Institute of British Architects, the Royal Institution of Chartered Surveyors or the Chartered Institute of Arbitrators. If the appointor is not selected in the appendix it provides for the President or a Vice President of the Royal Institute of British Architects to make the appointment.

The parties should endeavour to agree a named arbitrator wherever possible. In practice the party serving the written notice (the claimant) will often include a list of three or four names as possible arbitrators and invite the other party (the respondent) to agree to one of them, perhaps adding that in the absence of agreement to one of those names the respondent may wish to submit further names to the claimant for consideration. Sometimes, if the parties are hostile toward one another no names put forward will be agreed, so that the appointing body will have to nominate an arbitrator. The situation can sometimes become farcical especially where there is only a limited number of suitable arbitrators and the parties produce long lists which still result in no agreement. Although in such circumstances the appointing body could select an arbitrator even though named in the list, nevertheless they are likely to seek to avoid this, with a consequent serious reduction in the choice of arbitrators open to them. Where a claimant knows the other side to be hostile and likely to reject any names on the claimant's list, it is not unknown for the claimant to put on the list those arbitrators he does not want, thereby increasing the chances that those appearing in the respondent's list in response will include one of the names which the claimant would have liked in the first place. Such a tactical manoeuvre is obviously fraught with a serious risk of backfiring.

(4) Joinder of parties

Clause 41.2 tackles a potentially complex area of joinder of parties in arbitration where the disputes between the various parties are related.

Arbitration is consensual. Therefore a person who has not agreed to arbitrate cannot be compelled to. All of the JCT Arbitration Agreements are contained in contracts to which there are two parties. It is not unusual, however, for a dispute between the parties under one contract to affect a party under a related contract with one of the disputing parties. For example, an employer may be in dispute with a contractor regarding allegedly defective work. The contractor may likewise be in dispute with a nominated sub-contractor in respect of the same work. The contractor is a party to both the main contract and nominated sub-contract, but of course the nominated sub-contractor is not a party to the main contract, and the employer is not a party to the nominated sub-contract. Both contracts have arbitration agreements, but without more if the dispute were to be the subject of arbitration, it would necessarily result in two separate sets of arbitration proceedings in respect of the same issues – one between the employer and the contractor and the other between the contractor and the sub-contractor. There may be different arbitrators and different decisions made even though based upon the same evidence. If this potential problem arises in litigation the court has ample powers to bring all of the affected parties within the same proceedings so that the risk of inconsistent findings, as well as the duplication of costs, is avoided. The joinder provisions in the JCT Arbitration Agreements, such as the one in clause 41.2, are an attempt to achieve a similar result in arbitration with a resultant saving in time and cost.

These joinder provisions apply unless they are stated in the appendix to the contract not to apply.

Any number of potential difficulties can arise in the operation of these joinder provisions – see for example the attempt, fortunately unsuccessful, in the case of *A. Monk & Co Limited* v. *Devon County Council* (1978) (a tripartite arbitration between employer, main contractor and sub-contractor) to tie the hands of the main contractor in his dispute with the employer following a settlement between the main contractor and the sub-contractor. If co-operation and common sense prevail the problems are not insurmountable.

Clause 41.2.1 provides that if the dispute or difference falling within the Arbitration Agreement in 'this Contract' raises issues which are substantially the same as or connected with issues raised within the Arbitration Agreement in NSC/2 or NSC/2a; NSC/4 or NSC/4a or in any nominated supplier contract with the contractor (known as the 'related dispute') and if the related dispute has *already been referred for determination to an arbitrator*, then the employer and the contractor agree that the dispute under the Arbitration Agreement under this contract shall be referred to the arbitrator appointed to determine the related dispute.

It is important to be able to point to the precise moment when the related dispute was referred for determination to an arbitrator. The Arbitration Agreements in NSC/4, NSC/4a, NSC/2 and NSC/2a require the giving of a written notice by one party to the other, requiring the dispute or difference to be referred to arbitration. Clearly there is a time lag between the notice to refer and the appointment of an arbitrator taking place. Clause 41.2.1 refers to the related dispute having been referred to 'an Arbitrator' rather than simply referred to arbitration. It seems therefore that unless an arbitrator has actually been appointed in connection with the related dispute, the joinder provisions will not take effect. If such is the case it is possible to imagine situations in which one party would feel aggrieved by the manoeuvring of others. For example, the employer may give written notice to the contractor requiring a dispute to be referred to arbitration. The contractor may be unwilling to agree a named arbitrator so that appointment of an arbitrator has to be referred to the appointing body. Subsequently, and before the appointment is actually made, the contractor and sub-contractor may between them agree a named arbitrator who is then appointed. The employer must now accept this arbitrator. It could even be that the arbitrator was one put forward by the contractor to the employer and rejected by the latter.

Though the current wording of clause 41.2 is in some respects tighter than the earlier wording – see for example JCT 63 and the FASS 'Green Form' of Sub-Contract – some of the problems of the arbitrator's jurisdiction highlighted in cases such as *Higgs & Hill Building Ltd* v. *Campbell Dennis Ltd* (1982) and *Multi-Construction (Southern) Ltd* v. *Stent Foundations Ltd* (1988) could still give rise to difficulties.

By clause 41.2.2 there is to be no joinder to the extent that the employer or the contractor reasonably considers that the arbitrator appointed to determine the related dispute is not appropriately qualified to determine the dispute or difference under this contract. If one party takes this point, it is not at all clear how it is resolved if the other party takes the view that the arbitrator is appropriately qualified – perhaps that particular issue has to be dealt with by an arbitrator appointed under clause 41 to specifically determine this particular issue. In practice, if the arbitrator is appropriately qualified to deal with the related dispute which, by definition, raises issues which are substantially the same as, or connected with the dispute under 'this Contract', it will not often be the case that the arbitrator will not be appropriately qualified unless he is disqualified for a non-technical reason; for example if he is not a disinterested party so far as the employer is concerned.

If the joinder takes place there are a number of ancillary provisions which assist in the process of resolving the enjoined arbitrations including the following:

● The Rules apply to the dispute under 'this Contract'. In practice, as a result of the joinder there will often be a significant departure from the timescale set out in the Rules. Read too literally the Rules look, at some points, almost unworkable without modification in such circumstances.

• The arbitrator is given powers to give such directions and to make such awards as if the High Court procedure on joining defendants and third parties was available to all of the parties and to the arbitrator.

• The consent of the parties to appeals or applications on questions of law (dealt with later when considering clause 41.6 – page 23) is extended to all related disputes. However, there appears to be a possible gap in these consent provisions. The consent given to taking a point of law from the arbitrator to the High Court under clause 41.6 is a consent only to the other party to the contract, i.e. the employer or the contractor only, as the case may be. So the situation could arise where it is, say, a nominated sub-contractor who wishes to take up a point of law. He will no doubt have the contractor's consent under the Arbitration Agreement in NSC/4 or NSC/4a. However, under the arbitration Agreement in this contract, that is, JCT 80, the employer is not bound to consent to the nominated sub-contractor as opposed to the contractor taking up a point of law. The consent required under section 1 or section 2 of the 1979 Act which, if given, avoids the need to obtain the leave of the court to a party taking up a point of law, is that of *all* the parties to the reference. If the answer is that there is in truth two (or more) separate references to arbitration where joinder takes place so that in the example given only the contractor's consent is required, it makes this insertion of the consent provisions in relation to related disputes irrelevant and unnecessary. Further, the 1979 Act talks of the consent of all of the *other parties* to the reference rather than simply the other party which is some, albeit limited (as it could be referring to arbitrations arising out of contracts having more than two parties) indication that joinder of related disputes produces a single reference. It may have been sensible to add into clause 41.6 after the words '. . . that either party . . .' some such additional words as 'or any party to a related dispute'. The last inset in clause 41.2.1 could then be removed altogether.

(5) Restrictions on opening references to arbitration before practical completion

Clause 41.3 provides that a reference to arbitration cannot be opened until after practical completion or alleged practical completion of the works or termination or alleged termination of the contractor's employment under the contract or abandonment of the works, unless the parties otherwise agree except for the disputes or differences in relation to the matters referred to in clauses 41.3.1; .2 or .3 which can be opened at any time.

Presumably, the division between those disputes or differences which may be opened at any time, and those which must await practical completion or the other events mentioned, is intended to draw a line between those issues which are preferably resolved as soon as possible as they may have a direct bearing on the continuation of the contract, and those which can wait until after the work has been completed. If so there are two points to make.

Firstly, there are many matters not specifically referred to as falling within the matters which can be opened at any time, where the case for rapid resolution of the dispute is as strong, or even stronger, than disputes or differences relating to other matters which can be the subject of arbitration at any time. Examples are:

● Whether the architect has expressed any dissatisfaction within a reasonable time from the execution of unsatisfactory work (clause 8.2.2).

● Whether the architect has unreasonably withheld his consent to the removal of unfixed materials or goods (clause 16.1).

● Whether the architect has unreasonably withheld his consent to the contractor sub-letting any part of the works (clause 19.2).

There are many others.

Secondly, with some imagination it is possible to fit almost any conceivable dispute or difference into one of the specifically listed matters, especially the first three listed in clause 41.3.2 namely:

● Whether or not the issue of an instruction is empowered by the conditions.

● Whether or not a certificate has been improperly withheld.

● Whether a certificate is not in accordance with the conditions.

It may be surmised that the reason for seeking to postpone the opening of a reference until after actual completion or determination or abandonment of the works is because it may divert the parties from the task of completing the works and might also cause the parties to polarise which could effect relationships. In addition it may be seen by some as undermining the authority of the architect. It may be said against this that if there is a dispute or difference it should not be left to fester, particularly if one party feels a strong sense of injustice.

If these restrictions on opening up arbitration are in truth of any substance then clearly if the dispute or difference is otherwise suitable for the application of Rule 5 (procedure without a hearing) or Rule 7 (short procedure with a hearing) for the conduct of the arbitration, both of which are directed at obtaining a speedy resolution, it seems a waste of such speed if a party has to wait months or even years before the reference to arbitration can even get under way. Though, so far as Rule 7 is concerned, as it can only operate if the parties agree that it should apply, they will no doubt also agree to the reference being opened as soon as the dispute or difference arises, despite any restriction contained in clause 41.3.

All in all, there should be no such restriction on when an arbitration may be opened. There is no such restriction in relation to disputes or differences under the Intermediate Form of Building Contract (IFC 84) or in the Agreement for Minor Building Works.

(6) *Powers of the arbitrator*

Clause 41.4 expressly gives the arbitrator extensive powers including the following:

(i) *Rectification*

The arbitrator has power to rectify the contract so that it accurately reflects the true agreement made between the parties. It is probable that even without this express power to rectify, the scope of the wording of the arbitration clause. '. . . any dispute or difference as to the construction of this contract or any matter or thing of whatsoever nature arising thereunder *or in connection therewith* . . .' (Article 5) is sufficient to enable the Arbitrator to rectify the contract in many instances – see *Ashville Investments Ltd v. Elmer Contractors Ltd* (1987) discussed earlier at page 8.

Despite this express power to rectify, the arbitrator cannot finally decide on an issue as to his jurisdiction, for instance, whether the contract contains a valid arbitration clause. For example, if a dispute arose as to whether the contract should be rectified so as to carry a deletion of the Arbitration Agreement, the arbitrator, if he were to decide that the Arbitration Agreement was intended to be deleted and was to order rectification of the contract accordingly, would be confirming that he had no jurisdiction to act as there was no arbitration agreement from which his powers could emanate.

(ii) Directing measurements or valuations

The arbitrator can direct such measurements or valuations as may in his opinion be desirable in order to determine the rights of the parties.

(iii) Opening up reviewing and revising certificates, opinions, decisions, requirements or notices

The express reference in clause 41.4 to the opening up, etc., of certificates, opinions, decisions, requirements or notices must relate to those given in circumstances where the architect uses his professional judgment or discretion under the contract. In other words, the arbitrator's power to open up would not extend to what was in truth a decision of the employer through the architect, for example, to vary the works. In practice, it is the role of the architect which will be reviewed here, for example, decisions as to extensions of time, certificates relating to interim valuations, opinions as to whether defects have been made good so as to justify a certificate of making good defects and so on.

There is an express exception to the arbitrator's power to open up, etc. (probably inserted for the avoidance of doubt), namely the architect's decision to issue instructions pursuant to clause 8.4.1 in regard to the removal from the site of all or any work, materials or goods not in accordance with the contract. Where work, materials or goods are not in accordance with the contract the architect has a number of cumulative options open to him quite apart from requiring removal. These are set out in clauses 8.4.2 and 8.4.4; e.g. allowing the non-complying work to remain, or requiring opening up and testing. If the architect chooses to require removal, rather than one of the other options available, this decision cannot be reviewed in arbitration. However, the insertion of the prefatory words '. . . where clause 8.4. is relevant . . .' ensures that the architect's opinion that work, materials or goods are not in accordance with the contract remains subject to the opening up and reviewing powers of the arbitrator.

So far as architect's instructions are concerned, while the arbitrator clearly has power to determine whether they are validly issued in the sense of being empowered by the conditions – see for example clause 41.3.2 – he has no power to open up and review, etc., where the architect not only has the power but also has a discretion as to whether to issue the instruction at all, for example, as to the expenditure of a provisional sum.

The opening up and reviewing, etc., powers of the arbitrator have been held to give the arbitrator powers which a court does not possess. In the Court of Appeal case of *Northern Regional Health Authority* v. *Derek Crouch Construction Company Limited and Others* (1984) the point was argued as to whether the court had power to open up, review or revise any certificate, opinion or decision of the architect in the same manner as an arbitrator appointed under clause 35 of JCT 63, which is similar in this respect to clause 41 of JCT 80. It was argued before the court that where the parties chose to litigate rather than arbitrate, there was an implied term that the courts would have the same power as the arbitrator under clause 35. The Court of Appeal held that it was not necessary to imply such a term. Lord Justice Browne-Wilkinson said:

'. . . in my judgment the court's jurisdiction would be limited to deciding whether or not the certificate or opinion was legally invalid because given, for example, in bad faith or in excess of his [the architect's] powers. In no circumstances would the court have power to revise such certificate or opinion solely on the ground that the court would have reached a different conclusion since so to do would be to interfere with the agreement of the parties . . . The limit of the court's jurisdiction would be to declare inoperative any certificate or opinion given by the architect if the architect had no power to give such certificate or opinion or had otherwise erred in law in giving it.'

It is clear therefore that if either employer or contractor wishes to challenge the opinion or decision of the architect on its merits rather than based upon a contention that the architect was acting outside or in excess of his powers under the contract, the courts will not have the power to review the opinion or decision. The matter will have to proceed by way of arbitration. This provides either party to the contract with very powerful ammunition indeed in seeking to have stayed under section 4 of the Arbitration Act 1950 any court action initiated by the other party. Lord Justice Donaldson MR said as follows:

'. . . our view, if accepted, will virtually give any party a right of veto on any attempt to bypass the arbitration clauses. They will be able to point out that they are thereby being deprived of the benefit of the special powers of the arbitrator under those clauses and they will accordingly have a very strong claim to a stay under section 4 of the Arbitration Act . . .'

All of the express powers given to the arbitrator in clause 41.4 are, however, made subject to the following provisions:

- clause 4.2 (architect's instructions deemed for all purposes to be valid if no written request to concur in the appointment of an arbitrator has been given before compliance with the instruction);

- clause 30.9 (final certificate conclusive evidence as to certain matters);

- clauses 38.4.3; 39.5.3 and 40.5 (quantity surveyor and contractor's agreement as to net amount payable to or allowable by the contractor in relation to certain events triggering fluctuations (or in the case of clause 40.5 any ascertainment following agreement to altered methods and procedures) is deemed for all purposes of the contract to be the amount payable or allowable thereunder).

(7) Appeals on and applications to determine questions of law in the High Court

Clause 41.6 provides that the parties agree and consent under Sections 1(3)(a) and 2(1)(b) of the 1979 Act that either party:

'.1 may appeal to the High Court on any question of law arising out of an award made in an arbitration under this Arbitration Agreement; and,

.2 may apply to the High Court to determine any question of law arising in the course of the reference;

and the parties agree that the High Court should have jurisdiction to determine any such question of law.'

To appreciate the significance of this provision it is necessary to briefly explain the background. The 1979 Act severely restricted the ability of a party to an arbitration bringing before the court questions of law arising either during the course of arbitration or contained in the award of an arbitrator.

By virtue of section 1 of the 1979 Act an appeal on any question of law arising out of an award can be brought to the courts only with the consent of the parties; or with leave of the court. By virtue of Section 2 of the 1979 Act, in the case of an application being made by any of the parties requesting the court to determine a question of law arising during the course of an arbitration, such an application can be brought only with either the arbitrator's consent and the leave of the court, or the consent of all parties.

So far as appeals on point of law arising out of the award are concerned, section 1(4) of the 1979 Act provides that the High Court shall not grant leave unless it considers that, having regard to all the circumstances, the determination of the question of law concerned could substantially affect the rights of one or more of the parties to the Arbitration Agreement. In relation to applications to the High Court for leave to have a point of law arising during the course of the arbitration reference determined, the court is required by section 2(2) of the 1979 Act to have regard to the same considerations, but it must also be satisfied that the determination of the application might produce substantial savings in costs to the parties.

In practice the High Court also takes other factors into account in deciding whether or not to grant leave, and also in deciding whether or not to grant leave to appeal to the Court of Appeal against the High Court's refusal to grant leave under sections 1 or 2 of the 1979 Act.

The leading case setting out the guidelines to be followed is still that of *Pioneer Shipping Ltd and Others* v. *B. T. P. Tioxide; (The Nema)* (1981) in which Lord Diplock stated the principles in this way:

'My Lords, in view of the cumulative effect of all these indications of Parliament's intention to promote greater finality in arbitral awards than was being achieved under the previous procedure as it was applied in practice, it would, in my view, defeat the main purpose of the first four sections of the 1979 Act if judges, when determining whether a case was one in which the new discretion to grant leave to appeal should be exercised in favour of an applicant against objection by any other party to the reference, did not apply much stricter criteria than those stated in *The Lysland* which used to be applied in exercising the former discretion to require an arbitrator to state such a special case for the opinion of the court.

'Where, as in the instant case, the question of law involved is the construction of a one-off clause the application of which to the particular facts of the case is in issue in the arbitration, leave should not normally be given unless it is apparent to the judge, on a mere perusal of the reasoned award itself without the benefit of adversarial argument, that the meaning ascribed to the clause by the arbitrator is obviously wrong; but if on such perusal it appears to the judge that it is possible that argument might persuade him, despite impression to the contrary, that the arbitrator might be right, he should not grant leave; the parties should be left to accept, for better or for worse, the decision of the tribunal that they had chosen to decide the matter in the first instance. The instant case was clearly one in which there was more than one possible view as to the meaning of the one-off clause . . .

'For reasons already sufficiently discussed, rather less strict criteria are in my view appropriate where questions of construction of contracts in standard terms are concerned. That there should be as high a degree of legal certainty as it is practicable to obtain as to how such terms apply on the occurrence of events of a kind that it is not unlikely may reproduce themselves in similar transactions between other parties engaged in the same trade is a public interest that is recognised by the 1979 Act, particularly in section 4. So, if the decision of the question of construction in the circumstances of the particular case would add significantly to the clarity and certainty of English commercial law it would be proper to give leave in a case sufficiently substantial to escape the ban imposed by the first part of section 1(4), bearing in mind always that a superabundance of citable judicial decisions arising out of slightly different facts is calculated to hinder rather than to promote clarity in settled principles of commercial law. But leave should not be given, even in such a case, unless the judge considered that a strong *prima facie* case had been made out that the arbitrator had been wrong in his construction; and when the events to which the standard clause fell to be applied in the particular arbitration were themselves one-off events stricter criteria should be applied on the same lines as those I have suggested as appropriate to one-off clauses.

'In deciding how to exercise his discretion whether to give leave to appeal under section 1(2) what the judge should normally ask himself in this type of arbitration, particularly where the events relied on are one-off events, is not whether he agrees with the decision reached by the arbitrator, but: does it appear on perusal of the award either that the arbitrator misdirected himself in law or that his decision was such that no reasonable arbitrator could reach? While this should, in my view, be the normal practice, there may be cases where the events relied on as amounting to frustration are not one-off events affecting only the transaction between the particular parties to the arbitration but events of a general character that affect similar transactions between many other persons engaged in the same kind of commercial activity; the closing of the Suez Canal, the United States soya-bean embargo, the war between Iraq and Iran, are instances within the last two decades that spring to mind. Where such is the case it is in the interests of legal certainty that there should be some uniformity in the decisions of arbitrators as to the effect, frustrating or otherwise, of such an event on similar transactions, in order that other traders may be sufficiently certain where they stand as to be able to close their own transactions without recourse to arbitration. In such a case, unless there were prospects of an appeal being brought by consent of all the parties as a test case under section 1(3)(a), it might be a proper exercise of the judge's discretion to give leave to appeal in order to express a conclusion as to the frustrating effect of the event that would afford guidance binding on the arbitrators in other arbitrations arising out of the same event, if the judge thought that in the particular case in which leave to appeal was sought the conclusion reached by the arbitrator, although not deserving to be stigmatised as one which no reasonable person could have reached, was, in the judge's view, not right . . .'

Turning to the specific consideration as to whether the High Court should grant leave to a party to appeal to the Court of Appeal against the judge's refusal to grant leave under the 1979 Act, the principles to have in mind are those outlined in *Antaios Cia Naviera S.A.* v. *Salen Rederierna A.B.; (The Antaios)* (1984) in which Lord Diplock said in the course of his judgment:

'My Lords, I think that your Lordships should take this opportunity of affirming the guideline given in the *Nema* . . .

that, even in a case that turns on the construction of a standard term, "leave should not be given . . . unless the judge considered that a strong *prima facie* case had been made out that the arbitrator had been wrong in his construction" applies even though there may be dicta in other reported cases at first instance which suggests that on some question of the construction of that standard term there may among commercial judges be two schools of thought. I am confining myself to conflicting dicta, not decisions. If there are conflicting decisions, the judge should give leave to appeal to the High Court, and whatever judge hears the appeal should in accordance with the decision that he favours give leave to appeal from his decision to the Court of Appeal with the appropriate certificate under section 1(7) as to the general public importance of the question to which it relates; for only thus can be attained that desirable degree of certainty in English commercial law which section 1(4) of the 1979 Act was designed to preserve . . .

'It was strenuously urged on your Lordships that, wherever it could be shown by comparison of judicial dicta that there were two schools of thought among commercial judges on any question of construction of a standard term in a commercial contract, leave to appeal from an arbitral award which involved that question of construction would depend on which school of thought was the one to which the judge who heard the application adhered. Maybe it would; but it is in the very nature of judicial discretion that, within the bounds of "reasonableness" in the wide Wednesbury sense of that term, one just may exercise the discretion one way whereas another judge might have exercised it in another; it is not peculiar to section 1(3)(b). It follows that I do not agree with Sir John Donaldson MR where in the instant case he says that leave should be given under section 1(3)(b) to appeal to the High Court on a question of construction of a standard term on which it can be shown that there are two schools of thought among puisne judges where the conflict of judicial opinion appears in dicta only. This would not normally provide a reason for departing from the *Nema* guidelines which I have repeated earlier in this speech . . .

'This brings me to "the section 1(6A) question" canvassed in Staughton J's second judgment of 19 November 1982: when should a judge give leave to appeal to the Court of Appeal from his own grant or refusal of leave to appeal to the High Court from an arbitral award? I agree with him that leave to appeal to the Court of Appeal should be granted by the judge under section 1(6A) only in cases where a decision whether to grant or to refuse leave to appeal to the High Court under section 1(3)(b) in the particular case in his view called for some amplification, elucidation or adaption to changing practices of existing guidelines laid down by appellate courts, and that leave to appeal under section 1(6A) should not be granted in any other type of case. Judges should have the courage of their own convictions and decide for themselves whether, applying existing guidelines, leave to appeal to the High Court under section 1(3)(b) ought to be granted or not.'

Further refinement of the *Nema* principles has taken place in numerous cases. For example, in the case of *International Sea Tankers Inc.* v. *Hemisphere Shipping Co. Limited; (The Wenjiang)* (1982) Lord Denning said:

'In the ordinary way, on the application the judge will have the award before him and counsel to argue it. The judge should look at once to see if it is a one-off case. It may be one-off because the facts are so exceptional that they are singular to this case and not likely to occur again; or because it is a point of construction of a clause singular to this case which is not likely to be repeated. In such a case the judge should not give leave to appeal from the arbitrator if he thinks the arbitrator was right or probably right or may have been right. He should only give leave to appeal if he forms the provisional view that the arbitrator was wrong on a point of law which could substantially affect the rights of one or other of the parties.

'When the case is not one-off as so described, but it gives rise to a question of construction of a standard form with facts which may occur repeatedly or from time to time, then the judge should give leave if he thinks that the arbitrator may have gone wrong on the construction of the standard form: but not if he thinks the arbitrator was right.'

And in the case of *Petraco (Bermuda) Limited* v. *Petromed International S.A.* (1988) in relation to whether leave should be given in respect of a point of law not argued before the arbitrator, Lord Justice Staughton propounded the following additional guidelines for such a case:

(1) The fact that the point which it is proposed to argue is not argued before the arbitrator is not an absolute bar to the grant of leave to appeal.

(2) It is, however, to be taken into account in the exercise of the general discretion provided by section 1(3).
(3) Where the failure to argue the point below has had the result that all the necessary facts have not been found, this would be a powerful factor against granting leave.
(4) Even in such a case, it might be right in very special circumstances to remit the award for further facts to be found with a view to granting leave.
(5) If all necessary facts had been found, the judge should give such weight as he thinks fit to the failure to argue the point before the arbitrator. In particular he should have regard to whether the new point is similar to points that had been argued or whether it is a totally new and different point.

As can be seen therefore, the provision in advance of the consent of the parties in relation to appeals under section 1 or applications under section 2 of the 1979 Act potentially eliminates a very significant obstacle in the way of a party seeking to pursue a point of law before the High Court.

Given the background to the 1979 Act and its obvious intention to severely restrict the ability of a dissatisfied party taking a point of law to the High Court, the obtaining of the consent in advance of any dispute or difference arising by means of a provision in the Arbitration Agreement may be regarded by some as an attempt to circumvent the spirit if not the letter of the 1979 Act.

The case of *Finelvet A.G.* v. *Vinava Shipping Co. Limited (The Chrysalis)* (1983) is highly relevant here. In this case Mr Justice Mustill (as he then was) said:

'Counsel for the charterers has, however, contended that the position is different in the present case, because the parties had agreed in advance that there should be a right of appeal on any question of law. This shows, so it is maintained, that the parties wanted an authoritative ruling on the question of frustration and this they would not get from a mode of appeal which precluded the judge from substituting his own opinion for that of the arbitrator on the 'judgmental' stage of the reasoning process. I am afraid that I cannot read the agreement as showing any such intention. Its obvious purpose was to save the time and expense involved in a contested application under section 1(3)(b) of the 1979 Act . . .'

This last extract from the judgment of Mr Justice Mustill

appears to implicitly recognise that the consent in advance is adequate and effective under section 1 of the 1979 Act.

Even if the consent provisions in clause 41.6 were not to be accepted as a valid consent it may still have some effect upon the exercise by the court of its discretion in deciding whether to grant leave. For example, in the case of *Astro Valiente Compania Naviera S.A.* v. *Pakistan Ministry of Food and Agriculture (The Emmanuel Colocotronis)* (1982) Mr Justice Staughton (as he then was) said:

'. . . It was expressly agreed by both sides, at that time, that the arbitrators should give reasons in their award. That, under the 1979 Act, is tacitly an essential condition for there being an appeal to the court from an arbitrator's decision, because unless he gives reasons one cannot say whether it is right or wrong. So it does not look as though, at the time of that agreement, either party contemplated that the arbitrators' decision on this point should inevitably be final. On the contrary, it looks as though they contemplated at least the possibility that it would not be final . . .'

'Lord Diplock there (i.e. in *The Nema* case) says that leave should not be granted even in such a case unless the judge considers that a strong *prima facie* case had been made out that the arbitrators were wrong. I have said that I am unable to reach that conclusion, because this is a difficult and technical point on which I cannot reach a conclusion either way without benefit of argument and study of the authorities. However, I do not believe that Lord Diplock intended to lay down that as the sole and only test despite all other circumstances. In an earlier passage in his speech, to which counsel for the shipowners referred me, he said that it was legitimate and proper to take into account the circumstances in which the arbitration agreement was made. I have already referred to those circumstances, and to the fact that both parties, through their solicitors, agreed that the arbitrators should give reasons. That does not seem to me to show that the parties, or either of them, were determined, in the words of Lord Diplock, "to accept, for better or for worse, the decision of the tribunal that they had chosen to decide the matter in the first instance". It seems to be to show the contrary, as I have already said . . .'

Of course, even if consent given in advance is valid and effective, the courts here are looking at points of law only. There is always the very real risk that the courts may decide that the issue is really one of fact or mixed fact and law thus taking the issue outside of the 1979 Act altogether.

On an optimistic note, the consent provisions contained in the JCT Arbitration Agreements making it easier for the parties to take points of law to the High Court, coupled with the restrictions on the powers of the court in connection with opening up and reviewing and revising any certificates, opinions, requirements or notices of the architect, etc., thus pushing all such matters away from the courts and towards arbitration, could have the effect of leaving the courts, particularly those judges undertaking official referees' business (if appeals under the 1979 Act arising out of construction arbitrations are, as they seem to be, referred to them), somewhat freer to develop a body of case law relating to JCT contracts on a reasonably economic basis.

(8) *Appointment of replacement arbitrator*

Clause 41.8 contains a very useful provision dealing with the situation where the arbitrator dies or otherwise ceases to act. While in the absence of express provisions the High Court would have power to appoint a replacement arbitrator, nevertheless it is simpler and generally quicker for the original appointing body to re-appoint should the parties fail to agree a named replacement. The replacement arbitrator is bound by any directions or awards of the previous arbitrator to the same extent as a previous arbitrator would have been bound by his own directions or awards.

In arbitrations involving long hearings conducted under Rule 6 (full procedure with a hearing) the parties should give serious consideration to insuring the arbitrator against death or other incapacity from the beginning of the hearing to the publication of the award. Any need for a re-hearing would obviously cause great additional expense.

(9) *The JCT Arbitration Rules*

By clause 41.9 the arbitration is to be conducted in accordance with the JCT Arbitration Rules current at the *Base Date* stated in the appendix to the conditions though, as the clause goes on to state, the parties can if they wish, agree by a joint notice in writing to the arbitrator that the arbitration be conducted in accordance with any amendment of the rules published after the Base Date.

The arbitrator should, when appointed, always seek from the parties the Base Date in order to see which edition of the JCT Arbitration Rules apply, if there have been any amendments between the Base Date and his appointment, and bring this to the attention of the parties to see if they wish the amended Rules to apply, and if so to request from them their joint notice in writing.

Interpretation of the Rules

The Rules are a working commercial document regulating the conduct of any arbitration which is subject to them. They are not to be construed or interpreted as though they were part of a statute. This is particularly the case to the extent that the Rules are procedural in character. To the extent that the Rules deal with the powers of the arbitrator in relation to awards or orders rather than simple procedural matters, they may be subject to a somewhat stricter construction. It must always be remembered that the arbitrator is generally the master of the procedure to be adopted and the Rules are designed to regulate the procedures rather than to have any limiting or stultifying effect.

The JCT health warning

In footnote [y.3] to clause 41.9, it is stated that the Rules contain stricter time limits than those prescribed by some arbitration rules or those frequently observed in practice and that the parties should note that a failure by a party or the agent of a party to comply with the time limits incorporated in the Rules may have adverse consequences.

These strict time limits are discussed later when commenting upon the particular rules in which they appear. The parties and their representatives need to be aware of them. A failure to meet them could lead to the loss by a party of the opportunity to put its case. If the failure to comply with the time limits is due to ignorance on the part of a party's professional representative it could involve the representative in personal liability.

(10) Name borrowing arbitrations

There are occasions when by virtue of the NSC/4 and NSC/4a Form of Sub-Contract and, in fewer instances, the Form of Sub-

Contract NAM/SC and Works Contract/2, the main contractor is bound to seek from the employer on behalf of the sub-contractor the benefits which the contractor can obtain under the main contract which are in effect benefits the whole or part of which will enure for the sub-contractor. In NSC/4 and NSC/4a there are some express provisions entitling the sub-contractor to use the main contractor's name and requiring the main contractor if necessary to join with the sub-contractor in arbitration proceedings to enforce certain of the main contractor's rights and entitlements under the main contract where this will benefit the sub-contractor. See for example clauses 4.6; 11.3 and 21.7 of NSC/4 and NSC/4a.

In addition, there are certain standard forms of sub-contract (not produced by the JCT) for use with JCT main contracts, for example, DOM/1; DOM/2; IN/SC which provide that the contractor will, so far as he lawfully can, obtain for the sub-contractor any rights or benefits of the main contract in so far as applicable to the sub-contract works.

These provisions clearly require either expressly or impliedly that the main contractor will co-operate with the sub-contractor to enable a sub-contractor to obtain benefits or entitlements which will come from the employer. In a case concerning the name borrowing provisions in the FASS ('Green Form') of Sub-Contract for Nominated Sub-Contractors where JCT 63 is the main contract, namely, *Lorne Stewart Limited* v. *William Sindall Plc* (1986) it was held that there was an implied term in the sub-contract to the effect that (*per* His Honour Judge Hawser QC):

'Upon the sub-contractor exercising its right to use the main contractor's name in an arbitration against the employer, the main contractor will render to the sub-contractor such assistance and co-operation as may be necessary in order to enable the sub-contractor properly to conduct the said arbitration.'

This case is also instructive on such questions as the scope of discovery of documents by the main contractor and sub-contractor: the giving by an arbitrator of directions to the main contractor and the sub-contractor; and the degree of assistance and co-operation to be provided by the main contractor to the sub-contractor.

In the event of there being any disagreement between the main contractor and sub-contractor as to the claim which the sub-contractor wishes to pursue, which leads to a withdrawal of

reasonable assistance and co-operation on the part of the main
contractor, the arbitrator may well have to seek the assistance of
the court pursuant to section 12(5) of the 1950 Act or section 5 of
the 1979 Act.

Chapter 3

Rules of general application

Introduction

The Rules can be divided into those which are of general application and those which provide three different procedures for the conduct of the arbitration, namely Rule 5 (procedure without a hearing); Rule 6 (full procedure with a hearing); and Rule 7 (short procedure with a hearing). Details of these three procedures and the method by which they are selected (Rule 4) will be dealt with in subsequent chapters. This chapter concentrates on the remainder of the Rules which are of general application whichever procedure is adopted for the conduct of the arbitration.

Rule 1, which identifies the Arbitration Agreements in the various JCT contracts has already been dealt with at the beginning of Chapter 2.

Interpretation and provisions as to time

Introduction

As its heading indicates, Rule 2 deals with the meaning of certain expressions repeated throughout the Rules and also deals with certain provisions as to time. Included within Rule 2 is the description of the parties as claimant or respondent including where a joinder of parties takes place; the meaning to be given to 'Days'; 'Arbitration Agreement'; 'Notification Date'; 'award' and finally restrictions on the extending of time under the Rules.

Rule 2

2.1 The party who has required a dispute to be referred to arbitration is referred to as 'the Claimant'; the other party is referred to as 'the Respondent'. Where the Arbitrator has been appointed on a joint application the Arbitrator shall decide who will be the Claimant and who will be the Respondent.

2.2   The Claimant and Respondent are referred to as 'the parties' and this expression where the context so admits includes the Claimant and Respondent in any arbitration who have been joined in the proceedings under the relevant joinder provisions in the contract or sub-contract or other agreement referred to in Rule 1.

2.3   'Days' means calendar days but in computing any period of days referred to in these Rules all public holidays, the four days following Easter Monday, December 24, 27, 28, 29, 30 and 31 shall be excluded.

2.4   'Arbitration Agreement' means the relevant provisions of a contract, sub-contract or agreement under one of the contracts, sub-contracts or agreements referred to in Rule 1.

2.5   'Notification Date' means the date of notification by the Arbitrator to the parties of his acceptance of the appointment to proceed with the reference in accordance with the Arbitration Agreement and these Rules.

2.6   Where the context so admits 'award' includes an interim award.

2.7   No time required by these Rules, or by any direction of the Arbitrator, may be extended by agreement of the parties without the express written concurrence of the Arbitrator.

(1) Who are the parties to the arbitration?

Reference of disputes to arbitration is based on a contractual agreement to arbitrate. It is only the parties to the agreement to arbitrate or, where permitted, their successors or assigns, who may therefore be parties in the arbitration. By Rule 2.1, whichever party has required a dispute to be referred to arbitration, i.e. when one of the contracting parties gives written notice to the other requiring the dispute to be referred to arbitration, that person is to be referred to as the claimant with the other contracting party becoming the respondent.

However, Rule 2.1 goes on to provide that where the arbitrator has been appointed on a joint application the arbitrator shall decide who will be the claimant and respondent. However, the Arbitration Agreement (see Rule 2.4) does not expressly countenance such a joint application. Rather it envisages one party giving a written notice to the other requiring the dispute to be referred to arbitration. Accordingly, in all but exceptional cases, the person serving that notice will become the claimant and the party upon whom it is served the respondent.

The claimant and respondent are known as 'the parties' in accordance with Rule 2.2. This Rule also applies where the dispute is required to be referred to the same arbitrator as in a related dispute between one of the contracting parties and another party under a different contract where the joinder provisions operate. The joinder provisions have already been discussed – see page 15. In such a case there will be more than one set of claimants and respondents and any reference in the Rules to the parties will, where the context requires, include all sets of claimants and respondents in joined arbitration proceedings.

(2) The Arbitration Agreement

Any reference in the Rules to 'Arbitration Agreement' means the relevant provisions of the JCT contracts listed in Rule 1 (see page 6). This is consistent with the definition of 'arbitration agreement' to be found in section 32 of the 1950 Act which provides as follows:

'In this Part of this Act, unless the context otherwise requires, the expression "arbitration agreement" means a written agreement to submit present or future differences to arbitration, whether an arbitrator is named therein or not.'

(3) Days

Unfortunately the Rules nowhere refer to 'Days'. References are always to 'days' with a minuscule d. Presumably this is a mistake and in order to give 'Days' any meaning at all, the likelihood of such a mistake having been made will probably be recognised in interpreting the Rules. Days is to mean calendar days rather than working days. However, when calculating any period of days such calculation must exclude the following:

● public holidays,

● the four days following Easter Monday,

● December 24, 27, 28, 29, 30 and 31.

These excluded days are the normally accepted and recognised holidays within the contracting side of the industry, though less likely to be so treated by building owners and construction industry professionals in private practice.

(4) Notification Date

The Notification Date is the date on which the arbitrator notifies the parties of his acceptance of his appointment. This date effectively marks the beginning of the arbitration procedure as there will be an arbitrator in place and appropriate directions and timetables can be set. The Notification Date is expressly referred to in the following Rules: 4.1, 4.2.1, 4.3.2, 5.2, 9.1 and 9.2. In addition, though not expressly mentioned, the Notification Date is clearly relevant in relation to the operation of many other Rules, for example, Rule 4.2.2, 5.1.2 and 6.1.2.

Any delay in reaching the Notification Date could clearly delay any arbitration to be conducted under the Rules. A potential cause of delay is a failure by one or both of the parties to agree the arbitrator's terms of appointment. Particularly relevant here is the question of his fees. This could seriously impair the chances of the Rules achieving one of their main objectives, namely to reduce delays.

Where the arbitrator is appointed by the president or vice president of one of the appointing professional bodies, difficult questions arise of a contractual, moral and professional nature as to whether an arbitrator should accept an appointment where the question of his fees has not been agreed by the parties. If the terms as to his fees have not been agreed it will be implied that reasonable fees are chargeable. Rule 9 provides that as from the Notification Date the parties are liable to the arbitrator for his fees and expenses. Further, the arbitrator can render interim fee notes on a three monthly basis.

It is of the greatest importance that the arbitrator, upon accepting the appointment, confirms to the parties the date which he is to treat as the Notification Date. The timetable for the fixing of a preliminary meeting and/or the giving of directions as to which of the procedural rules – that is, Rules 5, 6 or 7 – is to apply is dependent upon establishing the Notification Date; and in turn the prescribed timetables for delivery of statements of case, etc., are geared to the date when the appropriate procedural rule for the conduct of the arbitration becomes applicable.

(5) 'award'

Any reference to 'award' includes as appropriate an interim award.

(6) Time

Where any time limit is referred to in the Rules or is contained in any direction of the arbitrator, the parties cannot agree to extend it without express written concurrence of the arbitrator. This fetter on the ability of the parties to extend any time periods by mutual consent is of major importance. Without the requirement that any extension of time is to be subject to the express written concurrence of the arbitrator, the arbitrator would have no power to control the timetable where this did not accord with the parties' wishes.

Some might say that as arbitration is a consensual process, with the arbitrator's authority stemming from the parties' agreement to arbitrate, it should be for the parties, in agreement, rather than the arbitrator, to decide whether time should be extended. The contrary case is that the essence of these Rules is that awards should be made and disputes resolved in the shortest reasonable time, and that the credibility of the Rules, as well as the reputation of arbitration generally in the building industry, could be brought into question if disputes are left to drag on.

It is true that at the present time, in litigation in the courts, the parties can almost always grant one another indulgences as to time which depart from the Rules of the Supreme Court or the court's own directions. However, even here there are limits, for example, adjourning a fixed hearing, where the court's consent is required. Further, it is likely that, before too long, radical reforms in civil procedures will give the courts far more direct control over the ability of litigants to please themselves as to the time for preparing their cases, on the grounds that the general benefit of speedy dispute resolution should on occasions overrule the wishes of the particular litigants. This is particularly important as the 'agreed' delays may not in truth be what the litigants, as opposed to their lawyers, actually want.

However, the arbitrator's power to control time by virtue of Rule 2.7 may if tested be more apparent than real. If the arbitrator refuses his consent when both parties agree that time should be extended, they can of course by agreement revoke the arbitrator's appointment. Where the parties regard the question of time as one of great importance the arbitrator may be unwise to refuse his consent though he may of course voice his disapproval.

Finally, Rule 12.2 provides that any non-compliance by the arbitrator himself with the Rules, including those as to time, for example, for giving his award, shall not of itself affect the validity of the award.

Service of statements documents and notices – content of statements

Introduction

Rule 3 covers firstly the service of statements, documents and notices under the Rules, and secondly the content of statements referred to in the Rules; namely statements of case, defence, reply and counterclaim.

Rule 3

3.1   Each party shall notify the other party and the Arbitrator of the address for service upon him of statements, documents or notices referred to in these Rules.

3.2   The service of any statements, documents or notices referred to in these Rules shall be

by actual delivery to the other party or

by first class post or

where a FAX number has previously been given to the sending party, by FAX (facsimile transmission) to that number.

Where service is by FAX, for record purposes the statement, document or notice served by FAX must forthwith be sent by first class post or actually delivered.

3.3   Subject to proof to the contrary service shall be deemed to have been effected for the purpose of these Rules upon actual delivery or two days, excluding Saturdays and Sundays, after the date of posting or upon the facsimile transmission having been effected.

3.4 Any statement referred to in these Rules shall:

> be in writing

> set out the factual and legal basis relied upon and

> be served upon the other party and a copy sent to the Arbitrator.

3.5 Without prejudice to any award in respect of general damages any statement of case or of counterclaim shall so far as practicable specify the remedy which the party seeks and where a monetary sum is being sought the amount sought in respect of each and every head of claim.

On occasions, there may be an issue as to whether a statement, document or notice has been served. It is convenient, therefore, to provide in the Rules for what amounts to proper service and also the effect of non-receipt.

(1) Service

(a) Address for service
Each party must notify the other party and the arbitrator of his address for service.

(b) Modes of service
Three methods of good service are provided:

- Actual delivery to the other party, presumably at the address for service, by properly leaving it there. It would appear sensible to endeavour to leave it with a responsible identified person who signs on a duplicate that the original has been received with the date and time being noted. Failing this, posting through the letter box will suffice. A note of the date, time and address should be made contemporaneously.

- First class post – the envelope should be correctly addressed and adequately stamped. If the time for service is likely to be crucial, consideration should be given to photocopying the envelope as addressed and stamped or franked with the date, time and place of posting together with a note of the contents endorsed thereon. The endorsement itself should be signed, timed and dated.

● By facsimile – provided a fax number has been supplied, service by fax is to be good service if sent to the correct number. Generally the fax machine will provide a printout of the details of the transmission including the time and date, the fax number of the destination for the transmission, the number of pages transmitted together with an indication of whether or not the transmission has been correctly effected. It should be noted that if service is by fax, a further copy must be sent forthwith by first class post or actually delivered for record purposes. This will provide some protection against the consequences of an imperfect transmission or of the facsimile copy fading with time. Clearly when there is a large number of documents service by fax is not a practical proposition. It may be that the arbitrator should consider at the outset agreeing with the parties that where service takes place by fax, any documents which are to be included with a statement of case, defence, counterclaim or reply shall be sent by first class post at the same time as the statement is faxed and that this should be regarded as effective service. This is particularly important as with the very tight timetables which are likely to operate under these Rules the facility of service by fax, if an address for service is at a distance, could well be of the utmost importance.

(c) Effect of alleged non-receipt

Unless there is adequate proof showing otherwise, service is *deemed* to have been effected either upon actual delivery, or two days (excluding weekends) after posting, or upon the fax transmission having been effected. The reference to two days will exclude public holidays, together with the other days noted in Rule 2.3, provided the mistaken use of a capital D in 'Days' is treated as a minuscule.

It seems odd to say the least that actual delivery is *deemed* to be effective service, subject to proof to the contrary. Actual delivery must be actual service rather than deemed service and there can be no proof to the contrary. Similarly with a fax which *has been transmitted*. The reference to 'proof to the contrary' is no doubt related to deemed delivery by post where clearly there may be proof of actual receipt which differs from the two day period stated in Rule 3.3.

It appears by virtue of Rule 3.2 and Rule 3.4 that the service by the arbitrator of notices upon one of the parties must comply with these service requirements. Whereas so far as the parties themselves are concerned, when they are required to send copies of statements to the arbitrator, these have to be sent rather than served – see the last line of Rule 3.4, from which it would appear that the service requirements do not apply in such a case. As the arbitrator, in the event of non-service or late service by one party on the other of a statement may, under the Rules, be required to follow a course of action which can crucially affect a party's position, the arbitrator should invariably direct that a copy of any statement is sent to him by first class post, fax or actual delivery at the same time as service on the other party takes place. He should also direct that the party who should have received a statement by a certain date and who has not done so should immediately inform the arbitrator of this fact or of late service, as the case may be.

(2) Statements of case, defence, counterclaim and reply

Rules 3.4 and 3.5 are crucial to the overall purpose of the Rules in bringing out the essential issues in dispute at an early stage which can speed up the process of resolution whether by settlement or otherwise. In addition it should make a significant impact in curtailing or eliminating the conventional process of discovery of documents which, in construction disputes, can sometimes be unnecessarily long-winded and expensive.

The more usual manner of reducing a claim or defence, etc., to writing is in the form of points of claim or points of defence, etc. These typically follow civil litigation pleadings. This is not what is required under the Rules. Indeed by definition ordinary pleadings will fail to comply with Rule 3.4 in that they should not (whereas the form of statement required by Rule 3.4 must) set out the legal basis relied upon, as well as the factual basis. Further, the statement must include a list of any documents which the claimant or the respondent, as the case may be, considers necessary to support any part of the relevant statement.

In the case of Rule 5 (procedure without a hearing) a copy of all of the listed documents must also be included with the statement (see Rule 5.3.6). Where Rule 6 (full procedure with a hearing) governs the conduct of the arbitration a copy of the principal documents on which reliance is placed must be included (see Rule 6.3.6). The question of relevant documentation is considered again when dicussing the three procedures and in particular Rule 5.3.6 (page 107); Rule 6.3.6 (page 119); and Rule 7.3 (page 130).

The result is that the usual process of discovery of documents by list and subsequent inspection which is often virtually automatic will not now as a rule be required.

Two points of particular relevance here are:

Firstly, the process of presenting relevant documents upon which it is intended to rely, together with the statement of case or defence, etc., will in appropriate cases, drastically reduce the number of documents which would otherwise be the subject of any discovery process.

Secondly, there is under the Rules no general obligation to give discovery of documents which are relevant to the case, but damaging to the party who has possession of them.

The consequent reduction in time and cost if the Rules are operated properly is much to be welcomed. It is to be hoped that this potential saving will not be lost by the giving of directions for discovery of all possibly relevant documents as a matter of course under Rule 12.1.7. This Rule is included in order to be used selectively.

There can be problems, perhaps more often apparent than real, in providing relevant documents in support of a statement of case, defence, etc., at the same time as serving the statement. It can result in more documents being produced than needs to be, as the statement is very often served when it is not or may not be appreciated whether any of the points made are accepted by the other side so as to eliminate the need for documentary proof. It could lead to the copying and including of documents which it turns out are not needed where an admission is subsequently made.

Arbitrators should seek as far as possible at the preliminary meeting to ascertain the areas of dispute, or more accurately the areas of agreement, particularly as to issues of fact. This will be necessary in any event in order to establish which of the three Rules, 5, 6 or 7 is the most appropriate for the conduct of the arbitration. The parties can and should of their own volition seek to isolate the factual and other issues which separate them and be ready to explain these in detail at any preliminary meeting so that the documentation required to support statements of case, defence, etc., can be accurately identified.

The drafting of conventional pleadings is something of an art. Unfortunately all too often understanding them is also an art. The idea behind the requirement for statements of case, etc., is that they will be both full and readily intelligible to non-lawyers. Clear and adequate statements of case should, if Rule 6 (full procedure with a hearing) is selected for the conduct of the arbitration, significantly reduce the length of opening statements at the hearing.

It may take some time for arbitrators, lawyers and others regularly representing parties to perfect this method of presenting a case in writing and in detail. On the one hand, it offers considerable flexibility, but on the other, any failure to think the issues through and then to express them in the statement clearly and logically could create a shambles. For the inexperienced or uncertain participant, the arbitrator should assist by exploring the issues at the preliminary meeting and perhaps suggesting at least the appropriate skeleton layout for the statements. Examples of simplified skeletons of statements are contained in Appendix 3 to this book. In practice the statements are likely to be quite detailed.

The arbitrator has power to order further documents to be supplied where he considers these essential to properly decide matters in dispute where either Rule 5 (procedure without a hearing – see Rule 5.8) or Rule 7 (short procedure with a hearing – see Rule 7.4) apply. There is no equivalent provision where Rule 6 (full procedure with a hearing) applies and this may be an accidental omission in the Rules. If it is an omission no doubt the problem can be solved by the arbitrator's use of the express power in Rule 12.1.7 to order any party to produce any documents or class of documents in his possession, power or custody which the arbitrator considers relevant.

Inspection by the arbitrator

Background law and practice

Even without an express provision in an arbitration agreement or arbitration rules to such effect, in many instances an implied term will exist enabling the arbitrator to inspect relevant work goods or materials. Further, it may be included within the powers given in section 12(1) of the 1950 Act which provides that the parties to the reference shall do '. . . all . . . things which during the proceedings on the reference the arbitrator . . . may require'.

Unless the arbitration agreement or applicable rules expressly provide that the arbitrator can decide the dispute without receiving evidence, and the JCT Arbitration Rules do not, the inspection is not itself evidence and does not avoid the necessity for receiving evidence. If therefore the arbitrator forms a certain view as a result of his inspection which differs from the evidence given before him, he must raise the point expressly and then allow the parties full and proper opportunity to consider his view and respond to it – In the case of *Fox* v. *P.G. Wellfair Limited* (1981) Lord Justice Dunn said:

> 'If the expert arbitrator, as he may be entitled to do, forms a view of the facts different from that given in the evidence which might produce a contrary result to that which emerges from the evidence, then he should bring that view to the attention of the parties. This is especially so where there is only one party and the arbitrator is, in effect, putting the alternative case for the party not present at the arbitration.
>
> Similarly, if an arbitrator as a result of a view of the premises reaches a conclusion contrary to or inconsistent with the evidence given at the hearing, then before incorporating that conclusion in his award he should bring it to the attention of the parties so that they may have an opportunity of dealing with it.'

In addition to any implied terms and the possible application of section 12(1) of the 1950 Act, application may be made to the High Court under section 12(6) of the 1950 Act pursuant to which the High Court has power on the application of a party or the arbitrator, to, *inter alia*, make orders for the inspection of any property or thing which is the subject of the reference, or as to which any question may arise therein and to authorise for this purpose any persons to enter upon or into any land or building in the possession of any party to the reference. The court may also authorise samples to be taken, observations to be made or experiments to be carried out, which may be necessary or expedient for the purpose of obtaining full information or evidence.

Rule 8

8.1 The Arbitrator may inspect any relevant work, goods or materials whether on the site or elsewhere. Such inspection shall not be treated as a hearing of the dispute.

8.2 Where under Rule 8.1 the Arbitrator has decided that he will inspect:

> where Rule 5 applies, as soon as the parties have served all their written statements or the last of the times for such service allowed by these Rules has expired the Arbitrator shall fix a date not more than 10 days in advance for his inspection and shall inform the parties of the date and time selected;

> where Rule 6 or Rule 7 applies, the Arbitrator shall fix a date for his inspection and shall inform the parties of the date and time selected.

8.3 **.1** The Arbitrator may require the Claimant or the Respondent, or person appointed on behalf of either of them, to attend the inspection solely for the purpose of identifying relevant work, goods or materials.

> **.2** No other person may attend the Arbitrator's inspection unless the Arbitrator shall otherwise direct.

The Rules provide that the arbitrator may inspect any relevant work, goods or materials whether on or off site. The item to be inspected may not only be the item in dispute, but could be other items inspected for purposes of making comparisons, for example, whether tiles are colour matched.

Depending upon the reason for the inspection, it may be appropriate for the arbitrator to seek the agreement of the parties, and to use his own skill and knowledge by treating his inspection as evidence in itself; for example, in a quality dispute under Rule 7 (short procedure with a hearing). Unless express authority is obtained in this way the purpose of an inspection will be to simply enable the arbitrator to better understand the evidence being presented to him.

An inspection is obviously sensible where it is likely to save the time of the parties and the arbitrator in avoiding detailed written or oral descriptions.

Whilst an inspection will not take the place of a hearing, the hearing can in suitable cases take place immediately before, during or after the inspection.

Inspection where Rule 5 (procedure without a hearing) applies

When an arbitration is based on written submissions, i.e. documents only, the arbitrator will fix a date for the inspection immediately after service of the last statement (or the expiry of the final time limit in respect thereof). The date for the inspection must be fixed to take place not more than ten days ahead and the arbitrator must of course inform the parties of the date and time selected – Rule 8.2.

Inspection where Rule 6 (full procedure with a hearing) or Rule 7 (short procedure with a hearing) applies

Here the arbitrator fixes a convenient date for the inspection. The Rules provide no time scale in this instance (Rule 8.2).

Who should be present?

The arbitrator may require either party or both parties, or representatives of their choice, to attend purely for the purpose of identifying the relevant item. No one else may attend unless the arbitrator allows it. It is not therefore an occasion for the giving of any evidence, or the making of any submissions, unless the arbitrator and both parties specifically agree.

It is not absolutely clear if the effect of Rule 8.3 is that in the absence of a party being *required* to attend by the arbitrator, a party will have no right to attend the inspection. It would be most surprising if Rule 8.3.2 were to have this effect and it is suggested that based on principles of natural justice, as well as on a reasonable construction of Rule 8.3, the parties are entitled to attend and to at least observe the inspection.

The fact that the inspection by the arbitrator has a Rule to itself probably shows its significance in relation to such matters as quality disputes under Rule 7 (short procedure with a hearing).

Arbitrator's fees and expenses – costs

Background law and practice

(1) Arbitrator's remuneration

An arbitrator has a right implied into the arbitration agreement if not expressed, to reasonable remuneration for his services, including recovery of reasonable expenses. Furthermore, the usual practice is for the arbitrator not to deliver his award until his fees and expenses have been paid. He has a lien on the award for these. Thus in most cases which proceed as far as an award the arbitrator's position is reasonably secure.

The problems arise for the arbitrator where the parties settle, or where for some reason neither party wishes to take up the published award. In such a case the arbitrator will have to rely upon his express or implied right to remuneration. Any implied right to remuneration stems from the arbitration agreement, so that it is probable that both parties are liable for the whole of the arbitrator's reasonable remuneration.

Notwithstanding any implied right to remuneration, it is generally more satisfactory in practice for the arbitrator wherever possible to secure the express agreement of the parties to the terms of his remuneration before accepting the appointment. This has a number of advantages including the following:

• Where the arbitrator demands payment of his fees and expenses before delivery of the award, either party can, *if they have not previously agreed* the charges in writing, pay the sum claimed by the arbitrator into court and then apply to the court for an order for delivery up of the award and the taxation of the arbitrator's charges – section 19 of the 1950 Act. An agreement in writing as to fees and expenses will therefore avoid such a step being taken so far as the agreement goes. However, it may not prevent the application of section 19 altogether; for example, if the written agreement relates to an hourly rate, a challenge could still be made to the number of hours spent on the reference.

• The agreement as to remuneration can deal with cancelled hearings, for example, due to settlement. An arbitrator has to set aside time for a hearing and if it is cancelled by the parties at short notice the arbitrator may not be able to re-allocate that time productively. It is now common for arbitrators to provide for payment of a proportion of their charges in the event of a cancellation of a hearing. Provided any such calculation is a genuine pre-estimate of the loss of remuneration to the arbitrator it is probably not open to legal objection. However, except perhaps in relation to the cancellation at short notice of hearings lasting weeks or months, or where expenditure is actually incurred (for example, hotel booking deposit) the moral justification for charges where a cancellation takes place is often unconvincing.

● If the arbitration is likely to be protracted the question of interim payment of charges can be provided for.

● Provision can be made for the lodging of deposits as security for the arbitrator's fees either immediately upon appointment, or as a condition of it. Further, if appropriate, provision can be made for future deposits.

Liability of the parties between themselves for the arbitrator's remuneration
The arbitrator in his award should provide for the liability of the parties between themselves in respect of his fees and expenses as part of his order on costs.

(2) The costs of the reference

Unless the arbitration agreement provides otherwise the arbitrator will have a discretion as to the liability of the parties for costs of the reference – section 18 of the 1950 Act. While the arbitration agreement may seek to limit the arbitrator's discretion, care must be taken not to offend against the provisions of section 18(3) of the 1950 Act which provides that an agreement that a party shall, whatever the outcome, pay his own costs is void unless such agreement is made as part of an agreement to refer a dispute to arbitration made *after* the dispute has arisen.

Any costs directed to be paid by the award shall, unless they are to be taxed by the arbitrator, be taxable in the High Court – section 18(2) of the 1950 Act.

The arbitrator must deal with the question of costs in his award, except where it is an interim award and the costs are to be dealt with in a later award. Failure to address the question of costs will render the award defective and the court may remit it to the arbitrator for costs to be dealt with.

It is the duty of the arbitrator, subject to any contrary intention expressed in the arbitration agreement, to deal with costs which lie in the arbitrator's discretion – section 18(1) of the 1950 Act. If his award fails to deal with costs, either party may within 14 days of publication (extendable by the court) apply to the arbitrator for an order on costs. The arbitrator's discretion as to costs must be exercised judicially in accordance with the principles laid down in the case of *Donald Campbell and Company* v. *Pollak* (1927).

The arbitrator must not act capriciously when exercising his discretion. The general principle is that the party who is successful overall is entitled to have his costs. If the arbitrator in the exercise of his discretion departs from this general principle he should be able to point to a good reason connected with the case, and one which the courts could see was a proper reason.

The general principles were summarised by Mr Justice Mocatta in the case of *The Erich Schroeder* (1974) as follows:

(i) An arbitrator, like a judge, in dealing with costs must exercise the discretion invested in him judicially.

(ii) There is no need for an umpire or arbitrator, if he so exercises his discretion as to depart from the general rule, to state the reason why he does so in his award. On the other hand, in all probability, in most cases where an umpire/ arbitrator does so act, it would save costs if he were to state his reasons in his award. In that event, the parties would not be put to the expense of trying to ascertain what his reasons were and possibly moving the court to set aside the award.

(iii) If the award does depart from the general rule as to costs, but bears on its face no statement of the reasons supporting that departure, the party objecting to the award in that respect may bring before the court such evidence as he can obtain as to the grounds, or lack of grounds, bearing upon the unusual exercise of discretion by the arbitrator or umpire.

(iv) The above propositions apply to all categories of awards as to costs. That is to say, they apply to the extreme case in which the successful party has been ordered to pay all the costs of an unsuccessful party as well as the costs of the award, and also to a case in which a successful party has been made to bear his own costs and to pay half the costs of the award.

(v) There is a burden of proof upon the party seeking to set aside an award in relation to the decision of an umpire or arbitrator in relation to costs or seeking to have the award remitted so that the arbitrator or umpire may deal with the costs in a way other than that in which he originally dealt with them.

In the case of *Thyssen (Great Britain) Limited* v. *Borough Council of Afan* (1978) Thyssen made two claims arising out of a building contract. The first claim was for about £20,000 as damages and the second claim was £7,000 in respect of delay. The arbitrator rejected the first claim and awarded Thyssen less than half of the amount of their second claim. The arbitrator in his final award ordered that there should be no order for costs on either side. In other words each side were to pay their own costs. The Borough Council applied to the High Court for an order under either section 22 of the 1950 Act remitting the award to the arbitrator or, under section 23 of the 1950 Act setting aside the award of the arbitrator. At first instance, it was held that there was no misconduct of the proceedings by the arbitrator and that it would not be proper to set aside the award or remit it to the arbitrator. The court held this to be the case even though on the material which the court had seen it would not have made the same order on costs itself.

The Court of Appeal upheld the judgment of the court at first instance, and in so doing made the point that although there were two matters in dispute, on one of which Thyssens clearly lost and on the other in which it was only partly successful, there was nevertheless a single proceeding and the arbitrator was entitled to take an overall view and even though the outcome of that overall view was surprising that did not demonstrate that the arbitrator had misconducted himself in the sense of not applying a judicial discretion properly.

The effect of a sealed offer, or a 'Calderbank offer', may well have a significant bearing upon the liability of the parties for costs where the amount awarded is less than the offer. A Calderbank offer is an offer of a party to settle a dispute on the terms offered but made 'without prejudice save as to costs' or in some such similar manner. It must not be mentioned to the arbitrator until he has made his award on all matters except costs. The name derives from the matrimonial case of *Calderbank* v. *Calderbank* (1975) in which such a device was first approved by the courts.

When the arbitrator comes to deal with costs, the sealed or Calderbank offer can then be disclosed. Accordingly if an undisclosed sealed or Calderbank offer exists, the party who has made it should ask the arbitrator to deal with everything other than costs in an interim award, and then to hear the parties on the question of costs and to make a final award relating thereto.

If the person in receipt of the Calderbank offer is successful in gaining an award in his favour but has not obtained more than the value of the Calderbank offer, he may well both lose his own costs from the date of the offer and may also be ordered to pay the costs of the party making the Calderbank offer from the same date.

The parties may if they wish, in the arbitration agreement, provide for what is to happen on the question of costs, except that if the parties wish to agree that each or either of them shall bear their own costs, such a provision is void unless contained in an agreement made *after* the dispute has arisen – see, for example, Rule 7.1.2 (short procedure with a hearing) and Rule 9.3 of the JCT Arbitration Rules.

The arbitrator may follow the High Court practice in awarding costs on the standard basis or on a more generous indemnity basis – see Order 62 Rule 12 of the Rules of the Supreme Court. Costs on the standard basis require a reasonable amount to be allowed in respect of all costs reasonably incurred with any doubts being resolved in favour of the paying party.

Costs on an indemnity basis requires that all costs should be allowed except in so far as they are of an unreasonable amount, or have been unreasonably incurred, and any doubts are resolved in favour of the receiving party. If the arbitrator chooses to tax costs himself, it would seem that by section 18(1) of the 1950 Act the arbitrator may have a somewhat wider discretion as to the basis of taxing costs than that of a taxing master in the High Court.

Rule 9

9.1 From the Notification Date the parties shall be jointly and severally liable to the Arbitrator for the payment of his fees and expenses.

9.2 In an arbitration which continues for more than 3 months after the Notification Date the Arbitrator shall be entitled to render fee notes at no less than 3-monthly intervals and the same shall be payable 14 days after delivery.

9.3 The Arbitrator shall, unless the parties inform him that they have otherwise agreed, include in his award his decision on the liability of the parties as between themselves for the payment of his fees and expenses and, subject to Rule 7.1.2. on the payment by one party of any costs of the other party.

9.4 The Claimant shall, unless the Respondent has previously done so, take up an award of the Arbitrator and pay his fees and expenses (or any balance thereof if Rule 9.2 has applied) within 10 days of the notification given by the Arbitrator to the parties of publication of the award as provided in Rule 11.3.

Fees and expenses

The Rules provide that as from the Notification Date the parties are jointly and severally liable to the arbitrator for payment of his fees and expenses. Both parties are therefore liable for all of the arbitrator's reasonable or agreed fees and expenses. The arbitrator's award must, unless the parties have otherwise agreed, provide for which party is to bear the ultimate liability for his fees and expenses.

If the arbitration continues for more than three months the arbitrator can render interim accounts on a three monthly basis payable within 14 days.

When the arbitrator notifies the parties that his award has been published – see Rule 11.3 – he is at the same time to notify them of his fees and expenses. Thereafter, unless the respondent has already done so in order to get delivery of the award, the claimant must within ten days pay the arbitrator's fees and expenses.

If the arbitration is settled before the publication of the award, the parties must notify the arbitrator who will either issue an order for termination of the arbitration or, if requested by the parties and agreed by him, record the settlement in a consent award. In either case the arbitrator's fees and expenses must be paid upon notification that such order or consent award is ready for delivery.

Costs

Rule 9.3 requires the arbitrator to deal in his award with the question of the liability of the parties for costs of the reference unless the parties have agreed on this themselves in which case it will be sensible to record this agreement in the award in any event.

If the joinder provisions of the Arbitration Agreement have been invoked the arbitrator may deal with the question of costs in the joined disputes in the same manner as the High Court which has power to make such orders as to costs between plaintiffs, defendants, and third, and subsequent parties, as the justice of the case may require.

By Rule 12.1.5, the arbitrator has power, at his discretion, to direct that costs, if not agreed, shall be taxed by the arbitrator. Many arbitrators are unwilling in practice to tax costs themselves, preferring instead to leave the parties to tax costs in the High Court.

It is certainly the case that taxation in the courts can be technical and complex, but it is not inevitable that the arbitrator has to adopt precisely the same rules and techniques. The arbitrator's detailed knowledge of the reference may have the attraction of saving time and cost. It may be that the arbitrator would, in a more complicated case, wish, with the consent of the parties, to appoint a costs assessor to assist him. The Costs Arbitration Service of the Chartered Institute of Arbitrators can be of assistance here and generally on the question of costs.

Payment to trustee-stakeholder

Background law and practice

Once an award is published and delivered by the arbitator it can be enforced through the courts by the successful party. There may be, and very often is, a claim and cross claim making up the reference to arbitration. If the cross claim is in the nature of a set off which can also be used as a defence (and for disputes arising under the same contract this will often be the position) an award on the claim cannot properly be made unless the merits of the cross claim have been fully taken into account. For example, a contractor may claim in respect of the proper valuation of variations. The employer may cross claim that other work of the contractor, apart from the varied work, is defective and has involved the employer in costs in necessary removal and replacement, not only of the defective work, but of part of the varied work which was otherwise good, but which had to be removed as part of the replacement of the defective work. The arbitrator cannot simply value the variation as good work without taking into consideration the fact that it was of no value to the employer if it had to be removed and replaced.

The cross claim, though arising out of the same contract, may nevertheless be entirely separate, in which event different considerations apply. For example, the contractor may claim an extension of time and consequential repayment of liquidated damages and the employer may cross claim in respect of a latent defect appearing after practical completion and after the certificate of making good defects has been issued. The issues are separate and so could result in cross awards in favour of each party. In such circumstances it may be possible for one of the claims to be disposed of more quickly than the other. In other words, the arbitrator may be in a position to make a final determination on the claim, or on the unconnected cross claim, by way of an award.

In litigation cases the court, having given judgment on a claim or counterclaim has a discretion to order a stay on such terms as he thinks fit where there are special circumstances rendering it inexpedient to allow enforcement of the judgment – see, for example, Order 47 Rule 1 of the Rules of the Supreme Court.

If the arbitrator makes an award on a claim before making an award on the unconnected cross claim, or vice versa, does he have a discretion to stay enforcement of the award pending the outcome of the other claim? Unless the arbitration agreement gives this power the answer would seem to be no. The successful party has a contractual right to take action to enforce the award.

However, two points should be noted. Firstly, to summarily enforce the award the successful party must seek leave of the court to enter judgment under section 26 of the 1950 Act – see also Order 73 Rule 10 of the Rules of the Supreme Court (the award can also be enforced through the County Court). Section 26(1) of the 1950 Act provides:

> 'An award on an arbitration agreement may, by leave of the High Court or a judge thereof, be enforced in the same manner as a judgment or order to the same effect, and where leave is so given, judgment may be entered in terms of the award.'

There seems little authority indicating the kind of reason why leave might be refused. If there is a strong *prima facie* case that the award can be attacked as invalid in some way – that is, outside the jurisdiction of the arbitrator – no doubt leave would be refused. It seems, however, quite probable that the mere existence of an independent cross claim which is still awaiting an arbitrator's award would not be a ground for refusing leave to the successful party to enter judgment in terms of the award under section 26 of the 1950 Act. However, the words of the section providing that if leave is given the award may be enforced '. . . in the same manner as a judgment . . . to the same effect' should be noted. It seems at least possible therefore that the court might under Order 47 Rule 1 of the Rules of the Supreme Court stay the execution of the judgment pending the outcome of the cross claim if it forms the view that the existence of the cross claim amounted to a special circumstance rendering it inexpedient to allow enforcement of the judgment. The position is unclear.

Secondly, if the successful party actually sues on the award – that is – a failure to pay it, rather than seeking leave of the court to enforce it, any judgment given would of course be subject to the court's discretion to stay under the Rules of the Supreme Court.

It can be seen that the position is not entirely free from doubt. It is sensible therefore to provide for such situations expressly in the arbitration agreement, for example, by providing for a stay of enforcement of the award and/or the lodgement of the sum awarded with a stakeholder.

Rule 10

10.1   If the Arbitrator publishes an award in favour of the Claimant before he has published his award on all matters in a counterclaim by the Respondent, the Arbitrator upon application by the Claimant or the Respondent and after considering any representations by the parties may direct that the whole or a part of the amount so awarded shall be deposited by the Respondent with a deposit-taking bank to hold as a trustee-stakeholder (as described in Rule 10.3) pending a direction of the Arbitrator under Rule 10.2.1 or of the parties under Rule 10.2.2 or of the court under Rule 10.2.3.

10.2   The trustee-stakeholder shall hold any amount deposited as a result of a direction of the Arbitrator under Rule 10.1 in trust for the parties until such time as either

   .1   the Arbitrator shall direct the trustee-stakeholder (whether as a result of his award or as a result of an agreement between the parties reported to the Arbitrator or otherwise) to whom the amount deposited, including any interest accrued thereon, should be paid by the trustee-stakeholder; or

   .2   if the Arbitrator is deceased or otherwise unable to issue any direction to the trustee-stakeholder under Rule 10.2.1 and the Arbitrator has not been replaced, the parties in a joint letter signed by or on behalf of each of them direct the trustee-stakeholder to whom the amount deposited, including any interest accrued thereon, should be paid by the trustee-stakeholder; or

   .3   a court of competent jurisdiction gives directions.

10.3   An amount so deposited may, notwithstanding the trust imposed, be held by the trustee-stakeholder as an ordinary bank deposit to the credit of the bank as a trustee-stakeholder in respect of the party making the deposit pursuant to a direction of the Arbitrator under Rule 10.1 and in respect of such deposit the trustee-stakeholder shall pay such usual interest which shall accrue to and form part of the deposit subject to the right of the trustee-

> stakeholder to deduct its reasonable and proper charges and, if deductible, any tax in respect of such interest from the amount deposited.

This Rule applies where there are claims and cross claims. It does not expressly enable the arbitrator to stay enforcement of an award pending the outcome of a cross claim. However it effectively achieves this where there are cross claims still to be determined by empowering the arbitrator to require all or part of the amount awarded to be deposited by the respondent with a stakeholder. This can include any interest or ascertained costs comprised in the award. The purpose behind this Rule is clear. There may be valid claims and cross claims. The claimant's claim may be capable of being disposed of promptly and before the respondent's cross claim. If the respondent has to meet the award in favour of the claimant he may find that upon succeeding on the cross claim the claimant is unable to meet it, the sum paid over by the respondent having been dissipated.

It seems unfortunate that according to Rule 10.1 it is only the respondent who may be ordered to make the deposit. In other words this means of staying enforcement whilst securing the amount awarded is only available in relation to a claimant's claim and does not extend, as surely it ought, to the respondent's cross claim where this can be expeditiously be dealt with prior to the claimant's claim. It may be that this omission is accidental rather then deliberate, especially as it states that the claimant as well as the respondent can make the application to the arbitrator. There is no obvious reason why the claimant who could otherwise enforce the award would seek to have the amount awarded paid to a trustee-stakeholder.

A possible shortcoming in the operation of Rule 10 is that it could have been expected that the obligation on the respondent to make the deposit would be backed by the obvious sanction, namely the deposit with a stakeholder being made a condition of the respondent pursuing his cross claim. As the Rule stands, failure to make the deposit does not appear to be a bar to the respondent pursuing the cross claim. In such a case, the possible option for the claimant or the arbitrator of applying to the High Court under section 5 of the 1979 Act extending the arbitrator's powers may not solve the problem as orders under section 5 only enable the arbitrator *to continue* with the reference in default of compliance, for example, with the arbitrator's direction under Rule 10. It may just be possible to construe the words in section 5(2), namely:

'. . . to continue with the reference in default of . . . any . . . act by one of the parties in the like manner as a judge of the High Court might continue with proceedings in that court where a party fails to comply with an order of that court or a requirement of the rules of court.'

as enabling the arbitrator to continue dealing with the cross claim for the purpose of staying it pending compliance with the direction to make the deposit on the basis that this is what the court could do.

It would have been preferable for the Rules to have expressly provided for the respondent's deposit with the trustee-stakeholder to be a condition of his being permitted to pursue his cross claim.

The real teeth behind Rule 10, however, in its present form, is that if the respondent fails to make the deposit the arbitrator can simply issue a further direction, cancelling the earlier direction and leaving the claimant free to enforce the award on the claim in the ordinary way.

The deposit is to be made with a deposit-taking bank, that is, a bank which is authorised by the Bank of England (or is otherwise by statute empowered) to engage in the business of deposit taking. The Rule does not make it clear whether the arbitrator or respondent chooses the bank. The money is held by the bank in the capacity of trustee-stakeholder. In other words the bank holds the money as trustee for the parties subject to the terms of the trust set out in Rule 10.3.

Notwithstanding its trustee status the bank is by Rule 10.3 expressly authorised to:

- Place the money into an ordinary bank deposit to the credit of the bank as trustee-stakeholder in favour of the party making the deposit pursuant to the arbitrator's direction. Quite apart from these express provisions the bank has a right to apply the funds generally in its business pending the funds being applied for their ultimate purpose – see *Space Investments Limited* v. *Canadian Imperial Bank of Commerce Trust Company (Bahamas) Limited* (1986).

- Credit the usual interest which then forms part of the capital sum deposited.

- Deduct reasonable and proper charges.

- If deductible at source, to deduct any tax in respect of such interest.

Rule 10.2 provides for how the deposited money is to be subsequently dealt with namely:

● In accordance with the arbitrator's directions in which case the destination of the interest should also be stated. It seems quite likely from the wording of Rule 10.2.1 that interest will always be paid to the person directed to receive the capital.

● If the arbitrator is unable to give directions and has not been replaced, the parties can in a joint letter direct the trustee-stakeholder to whom the capital and interest should be paid.

● A court of competent jurisdiction, that is, the High Court, can be requested to give directions.

The award

Background law and practice

There are few legal formalities as to the form of an award. It must be a final determination of all outstanding issues in the reference unless it is an interim award as to a specified cause of action or head of claim in which case it must be a final determination of those matters.

The award must be sufficiently certain to be capable of enforcement. It could even be an oral award unless the arbitration agreement requires it to be in written form. However, it makes obvious sense for it to be written. In practice, awards generally follow a uniform format being signed by the arbitrator and independently witnessed and dated.

Unless the arbitration agreement expresses a contrary intention, the agreement is deemed to contain a provision that the arbitrator may make an interim award – section 14 of the 1950 Act. The interim award must specify the cause of action or head of claim involved.

Further, unless a contrary intention is expressed in the arbitration agreement, it is deemed to contain a provision that the award shall be final and binding. However, this is subject to any legal rights there may be to challenge the award. As to the rights of a party to challenge the award reference should be made to the standard text books on arbitration. The question of appeals and applications to the High Court on questions of law has already been considered in commenting on the JCT Arbitration Agreements in Chapter 2 – see page 23.

It is worth pointing out here that if there is any possibility that a party may wish to appeal to the High Court on a point of law arising out of the award, it will be necessary for a reasoned award to be given by the arbitrator. If a reasoned award is required, the arbitrator should be informed at the earliest possible time and in any event before the award is published.

A valid award is conclusive evidence as between the parties of the facts found by it. A finding of fact by an arbitrator will also be binding on the same parties in any litigation between them. In the case of *R.M. Douglas Construction Limited* v. *Welsh Health Technical Services* (1985) His Honour Judge John Newey QC said as follows:

'In the light of the cases I think it clear that court and arbitration proceedings between the same parties relating to the same subject-matter may exist at the same time. A finding of fact in one set of proceedings will be binding in the other.'

Having made his award the arbitrator is *functus officio*. His job is done. Exceptionally, despite this he has power, unless the arbitration agreement expresses a contrary intention, to correct the award in respect of any clerical mistake or error arising from any accidental slip or omission – section 17 of the 1950 Act. Of course the arbitrator may be further involved in the event of a successful challenge of the award; for example, where the court remits it to him for reconsideration under section 22 of the 1950 Act, or where the court requires him to give reasons or further reasons for his award in connection with an appeal on a point of law arising out of his award – section 1(5) of the 1979 Act.

Costs

The question of costs has been dealt with earlier in the discussion of the background law and practice to Rule 9 – see page 50.

Interest

The question of interest may have to be considered by the arbitrator in three different situations.

(1) Interest on the award from the date of the award

Section 20 of the 1950 Act provides as follows:

> 'A sum to directed to be paid by an award shall, unless the award otherwise directs, carry interest as from the date of the award and at the same rate as a judgment debt.'

Though the arbitrator has a discretion as to whether the award shall attract interest if left unpaid, he has no discretion as to its rate. It should be remembered that section 20 only deals with interest on the award as from the date of the award.

(2) Interest up to the date of the award

Unless the arbitration agreement otherwise provides the arbitrator may award *simple interest* as he thinks fit – section 19A of the 1950 Act:

> '(a) on any sum which is the subject of the reference but which is paid before the award, for such period ending not later than the date of the payment as he thinks fit; and
> (b) on any sum which he awards, for such period ending not later than the date of the award as he thinks fit.'

(3) Interest on sums paid before the arbitration proceedings have been commenced.

This is a difficult area. If the claim is in respect of what is called 'general damages' as a result of breach of a contractual obligation to pay, the arbitrator cannot award interest if such sum has been paid before the commencement of the arbitration proceedings however belated that payment may have been – see *London, Chatham and Dover Railway Company* v. *South Eastern Railway Company* (1893) and the case of *La Pintada* (1985).

However it is otherwise if the claim is for what is known as 'special damage' suffered as a result of the late payment. The damage is 'special' if, though it may not arise naturally and in the ordinary course of things from the breach of contract and therefore not be obviously in the contemplation of the parties, nevertheless, because of the particular knowledge actually possessed by the parties at the time of entering into the contract, it could be foreseen as the likely consequence of a delay in payment.

If the matter was approached from first principles, a claim for interest on payment made late in breach of contract would be a loss arising naturally from the breach being in the contemplation of the parties, i.e. it would form part of a claim for general damages. It appears that this is unlikely now to be treated as the correct position. However interest on late payment may be let in, at least in part, by treating it wherever possible as special damage.

For example, in the case of *Wadsworth* v. *Lydall* (1981) the parties entered into an informal partnership agreement which granted an agricultural tenancy to Wadsworth to live in the farmhouse and run the farm. Some years later, on the dissolution of the partnership, Lydall was to pay £10,000 to Wadsworth on being given vacant possession. On the strength of this Wadsworth entered into an agreement with someone else. However, when he vacated the farm the £10,000 was not paid. Some time later he was paid £7,200 which he used to meet part of his obligations in favour of the third party. He raised the balance of the money due to the third party by taking out a mortgage. The question arose as to the special damages of £335 which Wadsworth had to pay in respect of interest to the third party for late completion of a purchase. The trial judge had disallowed this interest. Wadsworth appealed to the Court of Appeal who allowed Wadsworth's claim for interest. The principle was stated by Lord Justice Brightman as follows:

'In my view the damage claimed by the plaintiff was not too remote. It is clearly to be inferred from the evidence that the defendant well knew at the time of the negotiation of the contract . . . that the plaintiff would need to acquire another farm or smallholding as his home and his business, and that he would be dependent on the £10,000 payable under the contract in order to finance that purchase.

. . . In *London, Chatham and Dover Railway Company* v. *South Eastern Railway Company* (1893) the House of Lords was not concerned with a claim for special damages. The action was an action for an account. . . . If a plaintiff pleads and can prove that he has suffered special damages as a result of the defendant's failure to perform his obligation under a contract and such damage is not too remote . . . I can see no logical reason why such special damage should be irrecoverable merely because the obligation on which the defendant defaulted was an obligation to pay money and not some other type of obligation.'

This type of approach has been considerably widened. See such cases as the *President of India* v. *Lips Maritime Corp* (1987) in the

Court of Appeal in which Lord Justice Neill stated the current principles as follows:

> 'What then is the present law as to the recovery of damages at common law for a breach of contract which consists of the late payment of money? I would venture to state the position as follows.
>
> (1) A payee cannot recover damages by way of interest merely because the money has been paid late. The basis for this principle appears to be that the court will decline to impute to the parties the knowledge that in the ordinary course of things the late payment of money will result in loss. I would express my respectful agreement with the way in which Hobhouse J. explained the surviving principle in *International Minerals and Chemical Corp.* v. *Karl O Helm AG* . . .
>
>> "In my judgment, the surviving principle of legal policy is that it is a legal presumption that in the ordinary course of things a person does not suffer any loss by reason of the late payment of money. This is an artificial presumption, but is justified by the fact that the usual loss is an interest loss and that compensation for this has been provided for and limited by statute."
>
> (2) In order to recover damages for late payment it is therefore necessary for the payee to establish facts which bring the case within the second part of the rule in *Hadley* v. *Baxendale*. In *Knibb* v. *National Coal Board* (1986) . . . Sir John Donaldson MR stated the effect of the decision in *President of India* v. *La Pintada Compania Navigacion SA* in these terms:
>
>> "From this (the decision) it emerges that there is no general common law power which entitles courts to award interest . . . but that if a claimant could bring himself within the second part of the rule in *Hadley* v. *Baxendale* (1854) . . . he could claim special damages, nothwithstanding that the breach of contract alleged consisted in the nonpayment of a debt."
>
> It may be said that the line between the two parts of the rule in *Hadley* v. *Baxendale* has become blurred so that the division has lost much of its utility. . . . But it is clear, as Staughton J.

recognised in the instant case, that the court must find the dividing line because it is only if the claim falls within the second part of the rule that the loss can be recovered.

(3) It is important to keep in mind that the question in each case is to determine what loss was reasonably within the contemplation of the parties at the time when the contract was made. As I understand the matter, the principle in *London and Dover Railway Co.* v. *South Eastern Railway Co.* in its modern and restricted form, goes no further than to bar the recovery of claims for interest by way of general damages. Thus, in the case of a claim for damages for the late payment of money the court will not determine in favour of the plaintiff that damages flow from such delay "naturally, that is, according to the usual course of things." *Hadley* v. *Baxendale.* But a plaintiff will be able to recover damages in respect of a special loss if it is proved that the parties had knowledge of facts or circumstances from which it was reasonable to infer that delay in payment would lead to that loss.

Moreover, I do not understand that, provided that knowledge of the facts and circumstances from which such an inference can be drawn can be proved, it is necessary further to prove that the facts or circumstances were unusual, let alone unique to the particular contract.

As I have stated earlier, the question in each case is to determine what loss was reasonably within the contemplation of the parties at the time when the contract was made. In dealing with this question the court will not impute to the parties the knowledge that damages flow "naturally" from a delay in payment. But where there is evidence of what the parties knew or ought to have known the court is in a position to determine what was in their reasonable contemplation. For this purpose, the court is entitled to take account of the terms of the contract between the parties and of the surrounding circumstances, and to draw inferences. In drawing inferences as to the parties' actual or imputed knowledge, the court is not obliged to ignore facts or circumstances of which other people doing similar business might have been aware'.

In the case of *Holbeach Plant Hire Limited* v. *Anglian Water Authority* (1988) it was held that financing costs (for example, in running an overdraft) associated with the hiring of plant and equipment and the purchase of materials and the payment of wages, were capable, if they satisfied the criteria set out in the *Lips Maritime* case referred to above, of being special damages and therefore recoverable provided there is evidence that the parties had such losses in contemplation or would have had they addressed the point at the time of entering into the contract.

Rule 11

11.1   The Arbitrator shall only give reasons for his award where and to the extent required by either party by notice in writing to the Arbitrator with a copy to the other party.

11.2   .1   The Arbitrator may from time to time publish an interim award.

.2   If in any interim award the parties are directed to seek agreement on an amount or amounts due but such agreement is not reached by the parties within 28 days of receipt of that award (or within such other lesser or greater period as the Arbitrator may direct) the Arbitrator shall, on the basis of such further appropriate evidence or submissions as he may require, publish a further award on the amount due in respect of any liability or liabilities set out in the interim award.

11.3   On publishing an award the Arbitrator shall simultaneously send to the parties by first class post, a notification that his award is published and of the amount of his fees and expenses (or any balance thereof if Rule 9.2 has applied).

11.4   An Arbitrator's award can be taken up by either party on payment to the Arbitrator of his fees and expenses. The Arbitrator shall forthwith deliver the original award to the party who paid his fees and expenses and shall simultaneously send a certified copy of the award to the other party.

11.5   If, before an award is published, the parties agree on a settlement of the dispute the parties shall so notify the Arbitrator. The Arbitrator shall issue an order for the termination of the arbitration or, if requested by both parties and accepted by the Arbitrator, record the settlement in the form of a consent award. The Arbitrator's fees and expenses shall be paid upon notification that such order or consent award is ready for taking up and on payment thereof the Arbitrator shall be discharged and the reference to arbitration concluded.

Reasoned awards

If a reasoned award is required by one or more of the parties, whether for the purpose of a possible appeal or otherwise, the arbitrator shall only give such reasons where and to the extent required by notice in writing from one party to the arbitrator, with a copy to the other party – Rule 11.1. Though Rule 11.1 does not expressly say so, it is probable that the notice to the arbitrator must be before the award is published as thereafter he will be *functus officio*. Certainly in any event early notice is desirable. If no notice is given and a party wishes to appeal to the High Court on a point of law arising out of the award, the appellant may be faced with having to seek an order from the court requiring the arbitrator to state reasons and the court will not so order unless there is some 'special reason' why such a notice was not given when it should have been – section 1(6) of the 1979 Act.

As has been mentioned previously – see page 23 – the Arbitration Agreement provides that each party consents under the 1979 Act to the other party taking a point of law to the High Court so that leave of the court to appeal is not required. Despite that consent, if no reasoned award was requested there is a real risk that the appeal would not get off the ground.

It appears from Rule 11.1 that the arbitrator cannot give reasons for his award except when required to do so. Many arbitrators prefer to give reasons. This could be done with the consent of the parties preferably recorded as part of the preliminary directions.

The parties should remember that any request must be in writing to the arbitrator with a copy to the other party. It is not sufficient to require it orally at the preliminary meeting even if thereafter recorded in writing by the arbitrator in a written order or directions.

It may be that a party only wishes part of the award dealing with a particular matter to be the subject of reasons and Rule 11.1 expressly provides for this with the words '. . . where and to the extent required by either party . . .'.

Interim awards

It is clear that the arbitrator can make any number of interim awards that may be appropriate. If an interim award on liability is made the arbitrator can direct the parties to seek agreement on *quantum* i.e. the amount due as a result of the finding in the interim award. In making such an interim award the arbitrator must be careful to ensure that he expressly finds sufficient facts to enable the *quantum* exercise to be properly undertaken.

If the parties cannot agree within 28 days of *receipt* of the award (or such other period as the arbitrator may direct) the arbitrator must publish a further award on *quantum* having considered such further evidence or submissions as he requires. It should be remembered that the time limit of 28 days or such other time as the arbitrator directs cannot be extended without the arbitrator's concurrence even if the parties themselves wish it – Rule 2.7. However, it is most unlikely that the arbitrator will refuse a consent application to extend time – see earlier at page 39.

Though the Rules do not appear to expressly countenance the possibility, it will clearly on occasions be appropriate and sensible to determine liability under one Rule, for example, Rule 5 (procedure without a hearing) whilst dealing with *quantum* under another Rule, for example, Rule 6 (full procedure with a hearing). As it is not expressly permitted under the Rules, if one of the parties objects to the conduct of the dispute being split between Rules in this way, it may be feasible for the arbitrator to direct that Rule 5 applies and once having delivered an interim award to then direct a change of procedure to Rule 6 under the power given to him in Rule 12.3.

Publication of award

On publishing the award the arbitrator must simultaneously by first class post, notify the parties of his having done so, at the same time telling them the amount of his fees and expenses. The award can then be taken up by either party on payment of those fees and expenses. To whoever pays the arbitrator's fees and expenses, the arbitrator must forthwith deliver the original award and send a copy at the same time to the other party.

Settlement before award

In very many cases the parties will settle their differences before the award is published. If they are minded to settle they should not forget to deal, as between themselves, with who is to be responsible for the arbitrator's fees and expenses as well as who is to be responsible for their own costs.

The parties must notify the arbitrator of any settlement, who in turn must issue an order terminating the arbitration or if requested by *both* parties and if he agrees, record the terms of the settlement in a consent award. The arbitrator's fees and expenses are then to be paid upon his notifying the parties that such order or consent award is ready. The matter of the arbitrator's remuneration has been considered earlier – page 48 and 54.

If a dispute is settled it is much tidier to have the arbitration formally determined by an order or consent award. In addition it gives the arbitrator a convenient mechanism for obtaining his fees and expenses. If the dispute is settled without the parties notifying the arbitrator he will, if he discovers the settlement, e.g. by enquiry of the parties, wish to seek his fees and expenses. He is still entitled to payment by virtue of Rule 9.1. A further option could be to get both the parties to confirm that they have settled, even if by telephone, with the arbitrator then recording this in an order and thereupon seeking his fees and expenses.

Provided the reference gets beyond the preliminary meeting stage the arbitrator should not be left in a position of having a long period of inactivity with the matter eventually dying off. Where Rule 5 (procedure without a hearing) applies Rules 5.4 and 5.5, dealing with non-compliance with the time-tables, prevent this from happening. Where Rule 6 (full procedure with the hearing) applies Rules 6.4 and 6.5 prevent it. Under Rule 7 (short procedure with a hearing) whilst there are no specific rules dealing with non-compliance, the whole procedure is quick and inexpensive and the arbitrator will be unlikely to find himself having spent a great deal of time for which he will have to chase his fees and expenses. In any event this situation can be avoided by requiring a reasonable deposit to be paid at the outset as a term of the arbitrator's appointment. In addition of course the arbitrator can, if the arbitration continues for more than three months after the Notification Date, render fee notes at three monthly intervals – Rule 9.2.

Powers of the arbitrator

Source of the arbitrator's powers

An arbitrator's powers may be found in either the arbitration agreement, including any arbitration rules which may be thereby introduced; by statute, most importantly the 1950 and 1979 Acts; or by custom or practice. In the event of any divergence between the express provisions of the arbitration agreement (including any applicable rules) and the 1950 Act, in most cases the 1950 Act provides that the express terms of any arbitration agreement will prevail.

Of prime importance is the arbitrator's powers to control the reference subject to the provisions of the arbitration agreement and linked to this, the procedures to be adopted. It is the duty of the arbitrator to determine the issues in dispute as expeditiously and economically as possible whilst following the rules of natural justice. If he is to seek this end his role should be positive rather than passive. This will for instance include the setting of realistic time-tables for any necessary steps and the ability and willingness to deal firmly with non-compliance with any time-tables. While the agreement and co-operation of the parties is always desirable there may be occasions where the arbitrator cannot remain friends with everyone.

The choice of procedures available under the JCT Arbitration Rules is discussed in following chapters of this book. But whichever procedure is adopted the arbitrator should maintain firm control. Lord Justice Roskill (as he then was) in giving the Third Alexander Lecture in 1977 (reproduced in (1977) *Arbitration* 4) said:

'Rule 1 is – keep control of the proceedings and don't let cases drift. Remember you are the masters of your own procedure, then never try to fit every case into the same procedural strait-jacket because some won't fit. Be flexible, as flexible as you can in trying to meet the wishes of the parties, but above all be firm, politely firm, especially about delay . . . Why is it that some arbitrators seem frightened to grasp the nettle and take control of the cases and show that delay will not be tolerated? We all, I think, have some inbuilt fear of doing an injustice if we refuse to accept an excuse for seeking further time for pleadings or discovery or a request, attractively if unjustifiably advanced, for an adjournment of the hearing. A judge may feel inclined to take the risk because there is always the Court of Appeal to direct him if he has gone too far in a particular direction. But in matters like this an arbitrator has for all practical purposes both first and last word and I often think he fears that if he is firm someone may thereafter accuse him in the courts of "misconduct", that dreadful word. I can understand the fear though I sincerely believe it to be unjustified. It has, I think, an historical basis and stems from the days when the courts were hostile to arbitrations . . . but I do not believe that any court would presume to criticise an arbitrator who was firm in dealing with disobedience to his orders, so long as he acted fairly.'

So firmness and fairness are the keys in controlling the reference especially in relation to departures from any time-table.

The arbitrator should be scrupulously fair in giving both parties full opportunity to present their case ensuring that they are also made aware of the opposing case and given the opportunity to meet the opposing case. Much of the procedure leading up to a hearing as well as the hearing itself is geared to this end; for example, delivery of pleadings or statements of case, disclosure of relevant documents, exchanging experts' reports, proofs of evidence and so on.

Any arbitration rules should therefore ensure that realistic timescales are set for the various steps and should provide for some degree of flexibility.

In conducting a reference the arbitrator should ensure that any communications to him by one party are immediately communicated to the other. The arbitrator not only must be fair but must clearly be seen to be dealing evenhandedly with the parties.

Fairness in dealing with evidence is especially important. Unless there is some well established custom or practice to the contrary, or the arbitration agreement provides otherwise, or the parties with the concurrence of the arbitrator agree otherwise, a party is probably entitled to an oral hearing to test the evidence of witnesses, and indeed where there appears to be disputed issues of relevant facts an oral examination of witnesses is the only realistic course to follow. However, wherever possible the extent of the oral hearing should be tightly controlled by, for example, written legal submissions, exchanges of experts' reports and by proofs of evidence of witnesses of fact before the hearing.

The arbitrator should remember always to notify both parties in good time of any hearing date fixed whether or not he expects the non-attendance of a party in any event. In fixing a hearing date the arbitrator should endeavour to consult both parties so as to try and fix a convenient date. However he should not over indulge the parties. He should be satisfied that the date fixed will give the parties enough time to prepare and will not result in a party being seriously prejudiced (for example, where a vital witness has an important surgical operation booked) rather than inconvenienced. For example, a party may have to change his lawyer or other representative due to the date fixed being inconvenient. Provided the case is not a particularly long and complex one on which the present lawyer or other representative has already done a great deal of work this is not a good enough reason to delay a hearing unduly. It is unlikely in practice that at the time of the fixing of a hearing date the lawyer or other representative, particularly if it is counsel, will have done very much work on the case.

More difficult to deal with is the request for an adjournment of the hearing made late in the day. Each application will depend upon its own merits. Clearly illness of a party, or of a vital witness, or of a party's lawyer, or other representative is likely to be a good reason.

Some express statutory powers

Section 12 of the 1950 Act provides that unless a contrary intention is expressed in the arbitration agreement it shall be deemed to contain the following provisions:

(1) That the parties shall submit to being examined by the arbitrator on oath or affirmation in relation to matters in dispute. Clearly therefore an arbitrator can adopt an inquisitorial role where this is an appropriate way to proceed as it may often be if the parties act in person without a legal or other suitably qualified representative.

(2) That the parties shall produce before the arbitrator all documents in their possession or power and do all other things which during the proceedings the arbitrator may require.

(3) That witnesses shall, if the arbitrator thinks fit, be examined on oath or affirmation.

Furthermore, unless the arbitration agreement expresses a contrary intention the arbitrator has power to:

(a) make interim awards – Section 14 of the 1950 Act;
(b) order specific performance wherever the High Court could do so (except under a contract relating to land or any interest in land) – section 15 of the 1950 Act;

(c) deal with costs at his discretion judicially exercised – Section 18 of the 1950 Act.

Two further points should be noted. Firstly, if a party fails to comply with an order of the arbitrator, the arbitrator or any party can apply to the High Court which may make an order extending the powers of the arbitrator to continue the reference in default of appearance, or of any other act by one of the parties in the like manner as a judge might continue proceedings where a party fails to comply with an order or requirement of rules of court – section 5 of the 1979 Act. This section is rarely used. Default is much better dealt with expressly by arbitration rules to which the reference is made subject.

Secondly, by section 12(6) of the 1950 Act the High Court has power to make the same orders relating to arbitrations as it has in relation to High Court proceedings covering the following:

(a) security for costs;
(b) discovery of documents and interrogatories;
(c) the giving of evidence by affidavit;
(d) examination on oath of any witnesses before an officer of the High Court or any other person and the issue of a commission or request for the examination of a witness out of the jurisdiction;
(e) the preservation, interim custody or sale of any goods which are the subject matter of the reference;
(f) securing the amount in dispute in the reference;
(g) the detention, preservation or inspection of any property or thing which is the subject of the reference or as to which any question may arise therein, and authorising for any of the purposes aforesaid any persons to enter upon or into any land or building in the possession of any party to the reference, or authorising any samples to be taken or any observation to be made or experiment to be tried which may be necessary, or expedient for the purpose of obtaining full information or evidence;
(h) interim injunctions or the appointment of a receiver.

To the extent that any applicable arbitration rules do not cover such matters, section 12(6) of the 1950 Act can clearly be of considerable benefit particularly those powers relating to security for costs and sampling or testing.

Rule 12

12.1   In addition to any other powers conferred by law, the Arbitrator shall have the following powers:

.1   after consultation with the parties to take legal or technical advice on any matter arising out of or in connection with the arbitration;

.2   to give directions for protecting, storing, securing or disposing of property the subject of the dispute, at the expense of the parties or of either of them;

.3   to order that the Claimant or Counter-Claimant give security for the costs of the arbitration or any part thereof, and/or for the fees and expenses of the Arbitrator, in such form and of such amount as the Arbitrator may determine;

.4   to proceed in the absence of a party or his representative provided that reasonable notice of the Arbitrator's intention to proceed has been given to that party in accordance with the provisions of these Rules, including if there is to be a hearing, notice of the date and place thereof;

.5   at his discretion to direct that the costs, if not agreed, shall be taxed by the Arbitrator;

.6   to direct the giving of evidence by affidavit;

.7   to order any party to produce to the Arbitrator, and to the other party for inspection, and to supply copies of, any documents or classes of documents in the possession power or custody of the party which the Arbitrator determines to be relevant.

12.2   Subject to the Arbitration Acts 1950 to 1979 any non-compliance by the Arbitrator with these Rules, including those relating to time, shall not of itself affect the validity of an award.

12.3   If during the arbitration it appears to the Arbitrator to be necessary for the just and expeditious determination of the dispute that a Rule for the conduct of the arbitration other than that previously applicable shall apply, the Arbitrator, after considering any representations made by the parties, may so direct and shall give such further directions as he may deem appropriate.

The specific powers given to the arbitrator under this Rule are expressed to be in addition to any other powers conferred on the arbitrator by law, many of which have already been mentioned above.

Rule 12.1 provides seven express powers:

(1) *Taking legal or technical advice*

The arbitrator must consult the parties before taking legal or technical advice though he does not require their agreement. Despite this express power, there must be some limits to the arbitrator's right to obtain legal or technical advice. So far as taking legal advice is concerned the arbitrator can almost certainly, even without the consent of the parties, take advice as to the conduct of the reference, and as to the general principles of law applicable in drawing up the award. However, it is for the arbitrator to decide questions of law and not simply to adopt without question the view of some legal adviser if he does not agree with it. The arbitrator should generally inform the parties as to the burden of the legal advice obtained so that they may address him on the point before he reaches a decision. The arbitrator should also generally be prepared to disclose the source of any legal advice given, and if it is in writing to disclose this also.

If a difficult and crucial point of law arises the parties may agree to seek a determination of it by the High Court under section 2(1) of the 1979 Act. A more expeditious and economical procedure may be for all concerned to frame the question of law in suitable terms and submit it to a lawyer, possibly Queen's Counsel, for a final determination.

If it is appreciated well in advance that the outcome may well depend upon a difficult question of law, the arbitrator may wish to consider seeking the parties' agreement to the appointment of a legal assessor to sit alongside the arbitrator.

Where the arbitrator wishes to seek technical advice the limit of his power to do so, if the parties, having been consulted do not agree to it, is more difficult and uncertain. If the arbitrator is expressly authorised to use his own skill and knowledge in reaching his decision in addition to or instead of basing his decision on the evidence adduced by the parties, he may consult others where necessary in order to decide the matter and may adopt the views of those others as his own if, having used his own judgment, he so decides.

However, where the arbitrator has to decide the issues purely on the evidence before him, as is generally the case under these

Rules, rather than rely upon his own skill and knowledge of the subject matter, the arbitrator is in a more difficult position and might not be able, without express power in the Rules, to take such outside technical advice. It should be stressed that under these Rules there is no express power for the arbitrator to decide issues in dispute based upon his own knowledge rather than upon the evidence placed before him. His skill and experience are therefore used to enable him to evaluate the evidence rather than to ignore it and rely upon his own knowledge. To so rely would in effect be to give evidence to himself and this he must not do. This matter has been touched on earlier when considering the arbitrator's power to inspect under Rule 8 – see page 45 and the case of *Fox* v. *P.G. Wellfair Limited* (1981).

If the arbitrator is unhappy with any of the technical evidence before him as a result of his own knowledge and experience, he should openly disclose his misgivings to the parties so that they and any of the technical experts can address the points raised and make any necessary submissions or adduce any necessary evidence to deal with it.

In the light of the absence from the Rules of any express right for the arbitrator to arrive at decisions based upon his own knowledge, the power under Rule 12.1 for the arbitrator to take technical advice is somewhat puzzling. Does it mean that the arbitrator is expected to rely upon his own findings outside the formal arbitration, or is the power limited to his seeking to merely better understand generally problems (for example, consulting a technical expert being in the same category as reading a technical publication)?

It would seem wrong in the absence of the agreement of the parties for the arbitrator to take such advice directly on the subject matter of the dispute. It conflicts with the usual requirement for the parties through experts or otherwise to put forward all necessary evidence upon which the arbitrator is to make his decision. If the arbitrator does take independent technical advice he ought in any event to disclose that advice to the parties and invite them to comment upon it.

(2) Directions for protecting, storing, securing or disposing of property at the parties' expense

This is clearly a useful power to have in appropriate situations; for example, securing or storing allegedly defective goods or materials by putting them into the custody of some independent third party.

It is to be regretted that the Rules do not provide expressly for sampling or testing of goods or materials which might have been a useful provision. In the absence of any such express power or the specific agreement of the parties, it would be necessary for a party who wished sampling or testing to be carried out to seek an order of the High Court to that effect under section 12(6)(g) of the 1950 Act.

(3) Claimant or counter-claimant to give security for costs of the arbitration and/or for the fees and expenses of the arbitrator

This as an important power. A successful respondent may find that the claimant is unable to meet the respondent's costs if ordered to pay them. It is in some respects similar to the power of the High Court to order a plaintiff or a counter-claiming defendant to provide security for costs in that in both situations it is a person pursuing a claim who can be required to give security rather than the person defending a claim.

A basic general principle in litigation is that a claimant has to assess the prospects not only of the success or failure of his claim but also of actually obtaining *recovery* of damages and costs if successful. This is a constant consideration in deciding whether to commence or continue proceedings. The plaintiff is in a position to make such an assessment whereas a defendant to a claim has no choice in incurring costs if he wishes to defend a claim made against him. He has been brought into court involuntarily. It is generally therefore regarded as a hazard of litigation which a plaintiff has to face, and security for costs will not generally be ordered against a defendant.

The basis upon which the court will order security for costs is covered by Order 23 of the Rules of the Supreme Court and by appropriate case law, particularly the leading case of *Sir Lindsay Parkinson and Co. Limited* v. *Triplan Limited* (1973).

The circumstances in which an arbitrator under Rule 12.1.3 can order security for costs are not set out in the Rules. It is submitted that so long as the power is not used perniciously or oppressively or so as to do an injustice, the basis of its exercise need not slavishly follow the High Court approach. However, it would seem sensible for the arbitrator to be fully aware of the basis of the exercise by the High Court of this power and to depart from those principles only for good reason. Similar comments apply in relation to the form and amount of such security.

A particular point to note is that security ordered against a claimant or a counter-claimant ought not, except in truly exceptional circumstances, extend beyond what are the applicant's costs in defending the claim. In other words, the security ordered should not be such as to give protection in respect of the costs of pursuing a claim or counterclaim rather than the costs of defending a claim or counterclaim as the case may be. For example, if a respondent not only defends the claimant's claim but raises a counter-claim, any security of costs ordered in favour of the respondent should relate only to his costs of defending the claimant's claim and should not generally extend to the costs of the respondent pursuing his own counterclaim. However, some degree of overlap between defending a claim and pursuing a counterclaim is likely to be inevitable. In litigation, security for costs cannot be ordered against a defendant or a plaintiff to the extent that he is defending a claim or a counterclaim as the case may be.

The reference in the Rule to '. . . the costs of the arbitration . . .' seems therefore to be too wide and would have been better being expressly restricted to the costs of defending the claim or the counterclaim as the case may be, though comparison with Order 23 Rule 1 of the Rules of the Supreme Court shows that that Order refers to the court ordering '. . . the plaintiff to give . . . security for the defendant's costs of the action . . .'

The Rule also refers to security for the arbitrator's fees and expenses which is sensible else a successful respondent to a claim or counterclaim may find himself having to pay these in the first instance, only to find that the other party is unable to meet an order that as between the parties the losing party pays them.

Of course, this Rule will be most useful where Rule 6 (full procedure with a hearing) applies. Indeed it would rarely if ever be applicable where Rule 7 (short procedure with a hearing) is adopted, not only because Rule 7 arbitrations would be likely to involve minimal costs but also because the arbitrator has no power to order costs except where there are 'special reasons' – see Rule 7.1.2 – and it will not be possible for the arbitrator to decide as to the existence of special reasons until the hearing has been completed and therefore the costs incurred.

While a defendant will rarely be required to provide security for costs in a court action, it is not so as to the amount in dispute. On occasions a defendant to a claim in court is ordered to pay the sum or part of the sum in dispute into court as a condition of being allowed to defend. This can be a very important device to take away from a defendant to a claim any cash flow advantage in delaying the day of judgment. The requirement for a defendant to pay the sum in dispute into court can often result in a settlement. It is a great pity that the Rules do not provide the arbitrator with this power which, provided its operation is carefully circumscribed to avoid injustice to an impoverished respondent with a meritorious defence, would help to remove one of the greatest current abuses of the arbitration system in the construction industry today.

(4) *Proceeding in the absence of a party provided reasonable notice has been given in accordance with the Rules*

Though an arbitrator has power to proceed to make his award in the absence of a party, it is clearly sensible to have an express power particularly, as in the case of Rule 5 (procedure without a hearing), there will be no actual hearing. Rule 12.1.4 probably overlaps to some extent with express provisions elsewhere in the Rules requiring rather than empowering the arbitrator to proceed where one party fails to take an appropriate step in the procedure – for example in Rules 5.4, 5.5, 6.4 and 6.5.

By section 5 of the 1979 Act the High Court can by order extend the arbitrator's power to continue with the reference in default of appearance, or of any other act by one of the parties, in the like manner as a judge of the High Court might continue with proceedings where a party fails to comply with an order of the court or some requirement of rules of court.

Much of the benefit of any such order is now covered by Rule 12.1.4 which will avoid the delay and expense in making an application to the court to give the arbitrator such powers. Indeed it seems that by virtue of this Rule in conjunction with those mentioned above, the arbitrator will be obliged in appropriate circumstances to strike out claims or to debar a party from defending a claim. Strong stuff indeed!

(5) *The arbitrator at his discretion may direct that the costs if not agreed be taxed by him*

This Rule has been briefly commented upon earlier in discussing Rule 9.3 – see page 54.

(6) Directions for the giving of evidence by affidavit

By virtue of section 12(6)(c) of the 1950 Act the High Court has power to order, in relation to a reference to arbitration, the giving of evidence by affidavit. Having an express power under the Rules is obviously sensible in avoiding any potential delay or cost associated with an application to the High Court to make such an order. However, its use in practice is likely to be quite limited. If facts are admitted this may well be shown on the face of the statements of case, defence, etc., and so will require no evidence at all.

An order to exchange proofs of evidence may also reveal agreements of fact so that no further evidence will be required. If the statements of case, defence, etc., reveal a dispute as to fact which any exchange of proofs of evidence does not resolve, the chances are that such dispute will require oral evidence to be given so that it can be tested by cross examination of the witness. In such a case evidence by affidavit is not sufficient. It may be that where a fact is not expressly denied by a party but is expressly 'not admitted' thus requiring at least some formal evidence to be given, evidence by affidavit would satisfy the party concerned. Even here it is probably more convenient for the arbitrator to give leave under the Civil Evidence Act 1968 for a written statement to be served. If a Civil Evidence Act statement is to be served it must satisfy the requirements of the Act.

A useful summary of what is required by the Act can be found at paragraph 34.4 in the *Handbook of Arbitration Practice* by Ronald Bernstein. If the statement is challenged, but nevertheless the party putting it forward still wishes it to be accepted in evidence, the arbitrator may, if he wishes, still accept it in evidence rather than require the witness to be called, but clearly its evidential weight is likely to be seriously impaired and the arbitrator should treat it with caution. If the statement is challenged the arbitrator should generally require the witness concerned to give oral evidence.

(7) Ordering a party to produce for inspection, and supply copies of, any documents in his possession, power or custody

The full listing and inspection of all arguably relevant documents in a party's possession, power or custody in relation to a typical building contract dispute can cause great delay and expense which in the event may well be unjustified. Building contracts often produce a mass of documentation much of which may be marginally relevant but most, sometimes almost all, of which, is not significantly relevant. The trial bundle of documents (which is itself often far bigger than it needs to be) is likely to be only a fraction of the listed documents. Further, there is often a blind adherence to tradition by the parties' lawyers who will list documents relating to issues which are admitted on the face of the pleadings and for which no evidence, documentary or otherwise, will be needed.

Whilst the power in this Rule is clearly appropriate, it should be used selectively. The statement of case procedure with any documents relied upon being listed or included with the statements should greatly reduce the need for discovery and should help concentrate everyone's efforts on the key issues even if occasionally a marginally relevant point is missed.

Apart from any express power in the Rules, the High Court has power under section 12(6)(b) of the 1950 Act to make orders in respect of discovery of documents. Further, under section 12(4) of the 1950 Act any party may sue out a writ of subpoena requiring any person to produce documents at any hearing before the arbitrator to the extent that it relates to any document which that witness could be compelled to produce at a trial in the High Court.

The unthinking use by an arbitrator of this power to order production of documents by its inclusion as a standard direction is one of the greatest threats to the attainment of the objective of the Rules, namely as speedy and economical resolution of disputes as is possible, consistent with the rules of natural justice.

With the use of statements of case, etc., including documents relied upon, it will generally be appropriate before considering the giving of a direction under this Rule, to await the completion of the service of those documents so that the need for any further documentation can be considered at that time between the parties and the arbitrator. The question of the further production of documents can then be considered when the issues and supporting documentation can clearly be seen.

Arbitrator failing to comply with the Rules

The Rules in very many instances require that the arbitrator 'shall' do something either with or without a time limit. Rule 12.2 provides that any non-compliance shall not of itself affect the validity of any award. This Rule is made expressly subject to the 1950 and 1979 Acts. Thus if the effect of the arbitrator's non-compliance amounts to his having misconducted himself or the proceedings, or where the award has been thereby improperly procured, the High Court may remove the arbitrator and set the award aside – section 23 of the 1950 Act – or if the misconduct is purely of a technical nature may remit the award to the arbitrator for further consideration – section 22 of the 1950 Act.

Rule 12.2 is sensibly directed at ensuring that the mere failure by the arbitrator to comply with the Rules whether as to time or otherwise will not enable a party to challenge the validity of the award on that basis only; that is, to claim that non-compliance with a Rule by the arbitrator necessarily renders the award invalid or defective. However, where the non-compliance is such as to evidence a disregard of the Rules by the arbitrator, his jurisdiction may be called into question. See also the discussion under the heading 'Non-Compliance by Arbitrator' in Chapter 5, page 106.

Arbitrator's power to switch procedures

By Rule 12.3, the arbitrator can change from one of the Rules for the conduct of the arbitration to another. This means that he can change between Rules 5, 6 and 7. As Rule 12.3 refers to the arbitrator's power to direct that a different Rule for the 'conduct of the arbitration' shall be used, this clearly restricts the rule to changes between Rules 5, 6 and 7 – see the introductory words to Rule 5.1; 6.1 and 7.1.

It is important that the choice of procedure is not irrevocable. It may well become apparent, for instance, that in an arbitration which is being conducted under Rule 5 (procedure without a hearing) there are disputes as to relevant fact which may not previously have been appreciated and the arbitrator's power to switch to Rule 6 (full procedure with a hearing) is clearly sensible. Though the Rules do not make it as clear as they might do, it seems highly likely that the arbitrator cannot direct a change from Rule 5 or Rule 6 to Rule 7 (short procedure with a hearing) as this last Rule applies only if the parties have agreed to it.

Though the Rules provide for the selection of only one of the three separate procedures, there is no reason why the arbitrator should not seek by direction to apply different procedures to different issues arising in the dispute. For example, a reference may be taking place under Rule 6 but it may still be sensible to hive off one or more of the issues to be based on written submissions under Rule 5, or alternatively, whilst retaining the general operation of Rule 6, to nevertheless direct that on certain of the issues written submissions with supporting documents only rather than oral evidence will be required; for example, on a question of the interpretation of an agreed Specification. However, to do this it may be necessary to get the agreement of the parties as it is not clear that Rules 5, 6 and 7 can relate to specific issues rather than to the conduct of the arbitration as a whole. Rule 12.3 could usefully be made clearer on this point.

In practice, where the parties have not jointly decided on which Rule shall apply so that the arbitrator has to decide between Rule 5 and Rule 6, he might well, if unsure, direct that Rule 5 shall apply and then, after studying the statements of case, etc., decide whether he should continue under Rule 5 or, alternatively after considering representations of the parties, to direct a switch to Rule 6.

Though it is for the parties alone rather than the arbitrator to select Rule 7 (short procedure with a hearing), having selected it the arbitrator has the right to direct a change of procedure to another Rule, though he should do his utmost not to do so against the wishes of both parties. He should use his best endeavours to convince them that it is necessary to switch. Ultimately however if the arbitrator is satisfied that a change in the appropriate Rule for the conduct of the arbitration is necessary for the just and expeditious determination of the dispute he should so direct.

Although Rule 12.3 appears to enable the arbitrator to direct a change at any time during the arbitration, he clearly cannot do so before Rule 5, 6 or 7 has been selected in the first place.

There appears to be nothing to prevent the arbitrator directing more than one change.

Once a change has been directed the arbitrator may give such further directions as he deems appropriate.

Chapter 4

Conduct of the arbitration – choice of procedures – which Rule

Introduction

The Rules offer three different procedures for the conduct of arbitrations; namely Rule 5 (procedure without a hearing), Rule 6 (full procedure with a hearing) and Rule 7 (short procedure with a hearing). One of these Rules will be selected in accordance with Rule 4.

After one of these Rules has been selected the arbitrator has power to switch to one of the other Rules (though probably not Rule 7 without the consent of the parties) – Rule 12.3.

Though the Rules provide for three different procedures there may be good reason in appropriate cases for mixing the procedures in relation to different issues within the same reference as this could significantly reduce the overall time and cost. The different procedures could run concurrently or consecutively. It would be unfortunate if arbitrators were to take the view that if, for instance, a matter of disputed fact relevant to one issue required Rule 6 (full procedure with a hearing) for its resolution, including the oral examination of witnesses, this should result in all issues in the reference being dealt with under the same rule. Rule 5 (procedure without a hearing) or even Rule 7 (short procedure with a hearing) may be an appropriate procedure for certain issues.

It is unfortunately not clear from the Rules whether in the absence of a joint decision of the parties – see Rule 4.2.1 and 4.2.2 – the arbitrator can, under Rule 4.3.1, direct that Rule 5 and Rule 6 shall both apply but to different issues.

Rule 4.3.1 refers to '. . . which Rule shall apply to the Arbitration . . .'. 'Rule' is stated in the singular and is expressed in the context of the arbitration as a whole, so that it could well be that under the Rules the arbitrator cannot split a reference in this way without the agreement of the parties. If such is the case, it is most unfortunate and may to some extent play into the hands of a procrastinating respondent.

However, even if because one particular issue involves a dispute of fact it is necessary to operate the procedures of Rule 6 (full procedure with a hearing), it is still possible for the arbitrator to reduce the overall time and cost by limiting the oral hearing to the disputed question of fact and to seek to have other matters, where there is no factual dispute – for example, differences in interpretation – dealt with by some form of written procedure.

Background law and practice

The choice of procedure generally is governed by the arbitrator acting under the applicable arbitration agreement and any incorporated rules. The Rules of the Supreme Court – see the Supreme Court Practice ('The White Book') – have no direct application to arbitration, though they are often used for guidance. They should not be slavishly followed.

The arbitrator must act within the arbitration agreement in accordance with the rules of natural justice. Provided he does this, he is master of the procedure. In devising a procedure where the arbitrator has a discretion, i.e. in the absence of applicable rules, he must have due regard to the basic rules of evidence, though all of the detailed rules of evidence do not have to be adhered to. For example, in the absence of agreement by the parties, or applicable provisions in any incorporated arbitration rules, or well established custom or practice to the contrary, contested issues of fact must be tested by oral examination and cross-examination with each party being given an adequate opportunity to participate in that exercise. In the case of *Chilton* v. *Saga Holidays Plc* (1986) Sir John Donaldson MR said:

> 'Both courts and arbitrators in this country operate on an adversarial system of achieving justice. It is a system which can be modified by rules of court; it is a system which can be modified by contract between the parties; but, in the absence of one or the other, it is basically an adversarial system, and it is fundamental to that that each party shall be entitled to tender their own evidence and that the other party shall be entitled to ask questions designed to probe the accuracy or otherwise, or the completeness or otherwise, of the evidence which has been given'.

Not only must the arbitrator consider the extent to which oral evidence will be necessary. He must also decide whether any other aspect of the oral adversarial system will be required, for example, oral opening and closing speeches. There is no doubt that, more and more, the courts are adopting civil justice procedures designed to compel a 'cards on the table' approach, for example, exchange of experts' reports and experts meeting before the hearing; exchanges of written proofs of evidence of witnesses of fact; written opening and closing speeches, most of which are designed to clarify issues before the hearing and/or shorten the oral content of the hearing itself. Arbitrators are likely to be supported by the courts in adopting such an approach.

The inquisitorial approach

If an arbitrator acts purely inquisitorially, he takes on the burden of investigating the differences or disputes on his own initiative, summoning the parties to provide or obtain information for him as he thinks fit. He might appoint his own expert, investigate alleged defects by physical inspection or even testing, forming his own view based thereon rather than relying upon the evidence called by a party.

One advantage of such a system is that it is very much the arbitrator rather than the parties who control the time-table. A purely inquisitorial, as opposed to adversarial, system would perhaps be too much of a shock to the system so far as construction industry arbitration is concerned. However, a mixed system has distinct advantages. Once the issues have been clarified by pleadings or statements of case, etc., and discovery (limited or otherwise) has taken place, the arbitrator can form a view of the issues in dispute and give a clear indication to the parties, after considering any representations they may have, as to the nature or the type of evidence he requires and how best it might be obtained. This does not mean that he can necessarily rule out evidence which a party feels it is necessary to introduce.

The key to a successful combination of adversarial and inquisitorial procedures is, yet again, for the parties and the arbitrator at the earliest possible time to have a good grasp of the issues and just as importantly to have actually thought about the issues in terms of appropriate procedures to resolve them.

So far as construction industry arbitrations are concerned,

unless the applicable arbitration agreement or any incorporated rules expressly provides for a departure from adversarial procedures culminating in an oral hearing, there is no doubt that the arbitrator can be in difficulties in seeking to depart from such procedures. If the parties are represented by lawyers, those laywers are likely to be used to civil litigation with its continued adherence to oral combat. It is only natural for clients to place themselves in the hands of their lawyers in relation to the running of the arbitration. In these circumstances the arbitrator can face an uphill task in tailoring the procedure to the particular dispute. For this reason some arbitrators request the attendance of the parties in person as well as their representatives at the preliminary and other meetings in order to gauge the parties' views (and not just the parties representatives' views) on any suggestions put forward. Clearly it can help enormously if there are arbitration rules which allow for and control the flexibility in procedures governing the conduct of the arbitration.

Before looking specifically at the three procedures for the conduct of arbitrations under the JCT Arbitration Rules, the liberty has been taken to conclude this general introduction with a quotation from the *Handbook of Arbitration Practice* by Ronald Bernstein where, at page 41, the author says:

'Mustill and Boyd state that unless the arbitration agreement expressly or impliedly authorises him to do so the arbitrator should not carry out his own investigations into the issues without the consent of the parties. It is rare for such a power to be conferred expressly by the arbitration agreement; but the practice in a particular field often confers it impliedly, e.g. 'look-sniff' arbitrations as to quality in the commodity trades.

As a matter of practice it is suggested that if the parties after due deliberation oppose a proposal by the arbitrator that he make investigations of his own, or appoint his own expert to investigate and report, he should withdraw the proposal. If one party supports the proposal, and the other opposes it, the arbitrator should proceed with it if, but only if, he is satisfied that it has specific and substantial advantages to the parties, and will not produce injustice to either, as compared with the traditional adversarial procedure. If he does so, he should state his reasons fully. It is thought that the court would be unlikely to interfere with a decision as to procedure arrived at in this way.

In any event the arbitrator should not make investigations of his own without telling the parties and giving them an opportunity to comment.'

Selection of applicable Rule and the preliminary meeting

Rule 4 deals with the holding of (or dispensing with) a preliminary meeting and the selection of the appropriate procedure for the conduct of the arbitration namely Rule 5 (procedure without a hearing); Rule 6 (full procedure with a hearing) or Rule 7 (short procedure with a hearing).

Rule 4

4.1   Not later than 21 days from the Notification Date the Arbitrator shall, unless he and the parties otherwise agree, hold a preliminary meeting with the parties at such place and on such day and at such time as the Arbitrator directs.

4.2   **.1**   At the preliminary meeting, or if the Arbitrator and the parties have agreed that no preliminary meeting be held then not later than 21 days from the Notification Date, the parties shall jointly decide whether Rule 5 (procedure without hearing), Rule 6 (full procedure with hearing) or, subject to Rule 4.2.2, Rule 7 (short procedure with hearing) shall apply to the conduct of the arbitration.

   .2   If the Claimant wishes Rule 7 to apply to the conduct of the arbitration he shall, within a reasonable time after the commencement of the arbitration and at least 7 days before a decision under Rule 4.2.1 is required, formulate his case in writing in sufficient detail to identify the matters in dispute and submit that written case to the Respondent with a copy to the Arbitrator and state that at the preliminary meeting he will request the Respondent to agree that Rule 7 shall apply to the conduct of the arbitration. A preliminary meeting shall be held and if at that meeting the parties so agree the provisions of Rule 7 shall thereafter apply and the Arbitrator shall issue any necessary directions thereunder; if at any meeting the parties do not so agree the Arbitrator shall issue a direction under Rule 4.3.1 as to whether Rule 5 or Rule 6 shall apply to the conduct of the arbitration.

4.3   **.1**   If the parties have not jointly decided under Rule 4.2 which Rule shall apply to the arbitration the Arbitrator shall direct that Rule 5 shall apply unless the Arbitrator, having regard to any information supplied by, and/or any representations made by, the parties directs that Rule 6 shall apply.

   .2   A direction under Rule 4.3.1 shall be issued within 28 days of the

Notification Date or, if a preliminary meeting has been held, not later than 7 days after the date of the preliminary meeting.

4.4 Whichever of the Rules 5, 6 or 7 applies to the conduct of the arbitration all the other Rules so far as relevant and applicable shall apply.

The preliminary meeting

The arbitrator must fix a preliminary meeting to take place not later than 21 days from his appointment, that is, the Notification Date, unless he and the parties by agreement either fix a later date or dispense with the preliminary meeting altogether.

As a general rule a preliminary meeting should be arranged in all cases, except where the arbitrator is satisfied that the issues are sufficiently clear and the procedure sufficiently certain that the parties are both able and willing to put their cases clearly and promptly and prepare as necessary for any hearing if one is to take place. This will often take the form of directions agreed by consent, but great care must be taken that this is not simply a ritual which has built into it seeds of unnecessary delay or involves unnecessary procedural steps being taken.

Arbitrators should think long and hard before agreeing to dispense with their preliminary meeting on the basis of agreed directions between the parties.

The arbitrator should not see his role as passive, rather it should be active. He should endeavour to ensure that the parties or their representatives are fully prepared and briefed to discuss the issues in dispute at the preliminary meeting. He should himself get to grips with the issues at the earliest possible stage. It is only a good grasp of the real issues which will enable the appropriate procedure to be adopted and employed.

Depending upon the procedure to be adopted for the conduct of the arbitration, the arbitrator can in consultation with the parties give directions as to the time-table for delivery of statements and any other matters if relevant such as:

- the exchange of experts' reports and the meeting of experts either before or after reports are exchanged and either without prejudice or on an open basis;

- the exchange of proofs of evidence of witnesses of fact;

- the preparation of plans, drawings, photographs, etc.;

● discovery of documents – such a direction should be aimed at a selective process of discovery if any additional discovery at all is required. Generally this is unlikely to be determined until after service of any relevant statements of case, defence, etc., except where one party satisfies the arbitrator that the other party is likely to have in his possession documents damaging to that other party's case which would not therefore appear in the documentation in support of the statement in which case the arbitrator may issue selective discovery on that basis.

There are many other possible directions and matters which need to be considered at the preliminary meeting. A very useful and comprehensive list of these is to be found in the *Handbook of Arbitration Practice* by Ronald Bernstein at paragraph 11.13. A check list has also been provided in Appendix 3 to this book.

It is often appropriate, where a hearing is to form part of the process, i.e. where the case is not to proceed on documents only, for a hearing date to be fixed at an early stage, together with an estimated length for the hearing. In any letter fixing the preliminary meeting the arbitrator should inform the parties that they must be in a position to assist in the formulation of such an estimate.

It is worth repeating that the preliminary meeting must not become an unthinking ritual. If a check list of possible directions is used by the arbitrator, he should nevertheless satisfy himself that there is good reason for giving a direction in relation to any particular matter rather than simply giving directions because it appears on the check list.

At the preliminary meeting the parties in one form or another are face to face and the arbitrator can and should use the occasion to make fairly detailed enquiries about the nature of the dispute. The arbitrator may consider requiring the parties themselves to be in attendance in addition to their appointed representatives.

Unless the parties have jointly decided under which Rule the arbitration will be conducted, the arbitrator must give his directions as to which procedure is to apply not later than seven days after the date of the preliminary meeting, or if no preliminary meeting is to be held, within 28 days of the arbitrator's notification to the parties of his acceptance of appointment, that is, the Notification Date.

The method of selection

If a preliminary meeting is held the parties shall jointly decide which procedure to adopt from Rules 5, 6 or 7.

If no preliminary meeting is to be held the parties must jointly decide on which procedure to adopt not later than 21 days from the Notification Date.

If the parties fail jointly to decide then the arbitrator is to direct that Rule 5 is to apply unless he forms the view that Rule 6 is more appropriate. He has no power to direct that Rule 7 shall apply in the absence of a joint decision to that effect from the parties as their agreement to the adoption of Rule 7 is required. If one party wishes Rule 7 to apply then he must comply with certain steps as follows:

(1) within a reasonable time of the commencement of the arbitration (see earlier Chapter 2 at page 13) and at least seven days before the preliminary meeting, he must formulate his case in writing in sufficient detail to identify the matters in dispute;
(2) submit the written case to the respondent;
(3) send a copy of the written case to the arbitrator;
(4) state that at the preliminary meeting he will be requesting the respondent to agree that Rule 7 should apply.

If at the subsequent preliminary meeting the parties agree to the application of Rule 7 it shall thereafter apply. If no agreement is reached then the arbitrator directs that Rule 5 or Rule 6 shall apply. If Rule 7 is to apply there must be a preliminary meeting – Rule 4.2.2.

Chapter 5

Procedure without a hearing – Rule 5

Introduction

Rule 5 provides for arbitration without a hearing. It is based upon documents only in the form of statements of case, defence, etc., with supporting documentation. It is, therefore, unsuitable where it is known from the outset that there is a serious dispute as to relevant matters of fact for which the appropriate method by which the arbitrator can determine the relevant facts is the taking of oral evidence from witnesses which is subject to appropriate cross examination.

This procedure is suitable where the issues in dispute are as to such things as the meaning or interpretation of agreed contract documentation; for example, a clause of a specification, or as to the legal interpretation of the documents, or an agreed set of facts.

There may well be situations where at the outset the parties are not too sure themselves as to any differences of fact or as to their relevance or significance. In such cases it may well be sensible to begin the arbitration procedure under this Rule and, in addition to the statements and documents required under the Rule, to also have a simultaneous exchange of proofs of evidence of witnesses of fact and, if appropriate, experts' reports (with or without a meeting of experts). The arbitrator and the parties can then review this evidence to establish the measure of agreement or failure to agree. It may be that the issues can be decided on the information then available. Alternatively, the arbitrator may have to give directions under Rule 12.3 changing the procedure to Rule 6, although the exchanging of proofs of evidence and experts' reports should have the result in any event of significantly shortening, perhaps dramatically, what would otherwise be the length of any oral hearing under Rule 6.

As ever the goodwill of the parties, together with a competent arbitrator, will enable this procedure to be used for many disputes as a speedy economical method of dispute resolution. In the absence of goodwill from one of the parties, a strong arbitrator is required to give Rule 5 any chance of being effective.

The Rule 5 procedure provides a clear role for lawyers in the preparation of statements of case, defence, etc. The issues need to be framed with precision whether they relate to questions of law or to the interpretation of contract documentation. As will be seen below, the time-table prescribed by Rule 5 is very tight, and lawyers, as well as the parties themselves, must be aware of this. Where there is a considerable amount of relevant documentation, extraordinary measures may be necessary in order to keep to the required programme.

Rule 5

5.1 Rule 5 applies to the conduct of the arbitration where:

    .1 the parties have so decided under Rule 4.2.1; or

    .2 the provisions of Rule 4.3.1 have come into effect and the Arbitrator has not directed that Rule 6 shall apply.

5.2 The times for service required by Rule 5.3 shall apply unless, at a preliminary meeting, or, if no preliminary meeting has been held, then within 28 days of the Notification Date, the Arbitrator, after considering any representations made by the parties, has directed any times for service different from those required by Rule 5.3 in which case the times stated in such direction shall be substituted for the times required by Rule 5.3.

5.3 **.1** The Claimant shall, within 14 days after the date when Rule 5 becomes applicable, serve a statement of case.

    .2 If the Claimant serves a statement of case within the time or times allowed by these Rules the Respondent shall, within 14 days after service of the Claimant's statement of case, serve

        a statement of defence to the Claimant's statement of case; and

        a statement of any counterclaim.

    .3 If the Respondent serves a statement of defence within the time or times allowed by these Rules the Claimant may, within 14 days after such service, serve a statement of reply to the defence.

.4 If the Respondent serves a statement of counterclaim within the time or times allowed by these Rules the Claimant shall, within 14 days after such service, serve a statement of defence to the Respondent's counterclaim.

.5 If the Claimant serves a statement of defence to the Respondent's statement of counterclaim within the time or times allowed by these Rules the Respondent may, within 14 days after such service, serve a statement of reply to the defence.

.6 The Claimant with

his statement of case and

any statement of setting out a reply to the Respondent's statement of defence and

his statement of defence to any statement of counterclaim by the Respondent

and the Respondent with

his statement of defence and

any statement of counterclaim and

any statement setting out a reply to the Claimant's statement of defence to any counterclaim.

shall include a list of any documents the Claimant or Respondent as the case may be considers necessary to support any part of the relevant statement and a copy of those documents identifying clearly in each document that part or parts on which reliance is or is being placed.

5.4 If a party does not serve a statement of

case, defence, reply to the defence, counterclaim, defence to the counterclaim or reply to the defence to the counterclaim

within the relevant time required by Rule 5.3 or directed under Rule 5.2 the Arbitrator shall notify the parties that he proposes to proceed on the basis that the party will not be serving the same unless within 7 days of the date of service of that notification the relevant statement is served. If within 7 days of the date of service of that notification the relevant statement is not received the Arbitrator shall proceed on the basis that that party will not be serving the same. If the relevant statement is subsequently served it shall be of no effect unless the Arbitrator is satisfied that there was a good and proper reason both why an application was not made within the time required by Rule 5.7.1 and why a statement was not served within 7 days of the service of his notice given under Rule 5.4.

5.5   If the Claimant either does not serve his statement of case within the time or times allowed by these Rules or if served it is of no effect by reason of Rule 5.4 the Arbitrator shall make an award dismissing the claim and ordering the Claimant to pay the Arbitrator's fees and expenses and any costs hitherto incurred by the Respondent.

5.6   Provided that where either party has, or the parties have, previously delivered to the Arbitrator a statement or statements setting out the matter or matters in dispute including the factual and legal basis relied upon together with the information where relevant required by Rule 3.5 and a list of any documents and a copy of those documents as required by Rule 5.3.6, the Arbitrator may direct that such statement or statements shall stand in place of all or any of the statements or documents to be delivered in compliance with the requirements of Rule 5.3.

5.7   .1   Subject to a written application by the Claimant or Respondent for an extension of times for service required by Rule 5.3 or directed under Rule 5.2 being served upon the Arbitrator before the expiry of the relevant time for service, the Arbitrator may in his discretion extend by direction in writing to the Claimant and the Respondent the times for service required by Rule 5.3 or directed under Rule 5.2 provided he is satisfied that the reason for the application was in respect of matters which could reasonably be considered to be outside the control of the applicant.

.2   A copy of any written application under Rule 5.7.1 shall be served upon the other party who may, within 5 days of such service, serve written comments thereon upon the Arbitrator and serve a copy thereof upon the applicant. In exercising his discretion under Rule 5.7.1 the Arbitrator shall take such written comments into account.

5.8   Where the Arbitrator considers that any document listed in any of the statements referred to in Rule 5.3 or in any statement to which Rule 5.6 refers requires further clarification by an interview with the parties or otherwise, or that some further document is essential for him properly to decide on the matters in dispute the Arbitrator may require such clarification or further document by notice in writing to the Claimant or the Respondent as appropriate and shall serve a copy of that notice upon the party not required to provide such clarification or further document. Such clarification by an interview with the parties or otherwise shall be obtained in accordance with the directions of the Arbitrator and such further document shall be supplied to the Arbitrator with a copy of [sic to] the other party by the Claimant or Respondent forthwith upon receipt of the notice in writing from the Arbitrator.

5.9 .1 The Arbitrator shall publish his award within 28 days

after receipt of the last of the statements and documents referred to in Rule 5.3 or

after the expiry of the last of the times allowed by these Rules for their service

whichever is the earlier.

.2 The Arbitrator may decide to publish his award later than the expiry of the aforementioned 28 days period and if so he shall, prior to the expiry thereof, immediately notify the parties in writing when his award will be published.

Selecting Rule 5

Rule 5 applies to the conduct of the arbitration where either:

● the parties have jointly selected it under Rule 4.2.1; or

● the parties have not been able to agree any of the procedures in Rules 5, 6 or 7 for the conduct of the arbitration and the arbitrator, in deciding on the appropriate procedure under Rule 4.3.1 has directed that Rule 5 shall apply;

● the arbitrator has switched to Rule 5 from Rule 6 or Rule 7 in accordance with Rule 12.3.

It is clear from Rule 4.3.1 that in the absence of agreement by the parties as to the Rule which they wish to apply, the arbitrator must direct that Rule 5 applies unless, having regard to the information and representations of the parties, he directs that Rule 6 shall apply. This is no doubt the reason why the selection of Rule 5 is expressed in a negative form in Rule 5.1.2. While the intention is clear, namely that in the absence of agreement of the parties or adequate information from or representations made by them, Rule 5 is to apply, this Rule may well be unsuitable. For example, if it subsequently turns out that there are relevant facts in issue requiring oral evidence to be given. No doubt in such a case the arbitrator would change the procedure from Rule 5 to Rule 6 pursuant to his powers to do so under Rule 12.3.

Rule 4 provides that where the parties agree to Rule 5 they are to do so at the preliminary meeting or, if no preliminary meeting is necessary, then within 21 days from the Notification Date.

If the parties have not agreed to Rule 5 or any other Rule the arbitrator, if he intends to direct that Rule 5 applies, must issue an appropriate direction not later than seven days after the preliminary meeting or, if no preliminary meeting is held, within 28 days of the Notification Date.

When does Rule 5 become applicable?

The time-tables for the delivery of statements of case, defence, etc., set out in Rule 5.3 operate from the date 'when Rule 5 becomes applicable' – Rule 5.3.1. It is important therefore to be able to identify that date particularly as the time limits are stringent.

Depending upon whether or not a preliminary meeting is held and whether the parties have agreed to Rule 5 applying, or the arbitrator has directed it, the time at which Rule 5 becomes applicable will vary.

This date will be as follows:

● where the parties have jointly decided that Rule 5 shall apply the date is either the date of the preliminary meeting, or where no preliminary meeting is held, it is the date of the parties joint decision made within 21 days of the Notification Date. The arbitrator should carefully record this date and confirm it to the parties;

● where the parties have not jointly decided so that the arbitrator has to give directions, the date is the date on which the arbitrator issues the directions, which will be either on a date within seven days of the preliminary meeting or, if no preliminary meeting is held, then on a date within 28 days of the Notification Date. It would be sensible for the arbitrator to make clear when directing which Rule is to apply the date from which he regards the Rule as becoming applicable for the purpose of the prescribed time-table.

As the start of the time-table under Rule 5.3 cannot commence until the direction is given and as that direction, if there is a preliminary meeting, is given some time between the preliminary meeting and seven days thereafter, the reference in the first line of Rule 5.2 to '*at* the preliminary meeting' should properly be '*following* the preliminary meeting'. It will not, of course, matter if the arbitrator gets the directions issued on the same day as the preliminary meeting takes place. In any event the directions should record the date on which Rule 5 becomes applicable. Where a preliminary meeting is held it is necessary to discuss not only whether Rule 5 or Rule 6 is to apply, but also to discuss whether, whichever Rule applies, the time-table set out in Rule 5.3 or 6.3 respectively should be altered so that the parties can be heard on the point and the direction issued following the preliminary meeting can then either provide that the prescribed time-table shall apply or, alternatively, that they are varied.

The time when Rule 6 becomes applicable is calculated in the same way for the purposes of the Rule 6.3 time-table.

Time-table for Rule 5 procedure

Rule 5.3 prescribes a time-table for service by the parties of their statements of case, defence, reply to defence, counter-claim and defence to counter-claim, and reply to defence to counter-claim. However, the arbitrator may 'at' (more accurately 'following') the preliminary meeting, or if no preliminary meeting is held within 28 days of the Notification Date, direct a different time-table, after considering any representations by the parties.

A table showing the prescribed time-table under the Rule 5 procedure as from the date when it becomes applicable is shown at page 99.

Whether the Rule 5.3 prescribed time-table applies or different times are directed under Rule 5.2, in certain circumstances, the times may be extended by virtue of Rule 5.4 and 5.7. Further, the time within which the arbitrator has to publish his award may also be extended – Rule 5.9.

Rule 5 – maximum prescribed time-table up to award if no extensions or abbreviations for delivery of statements

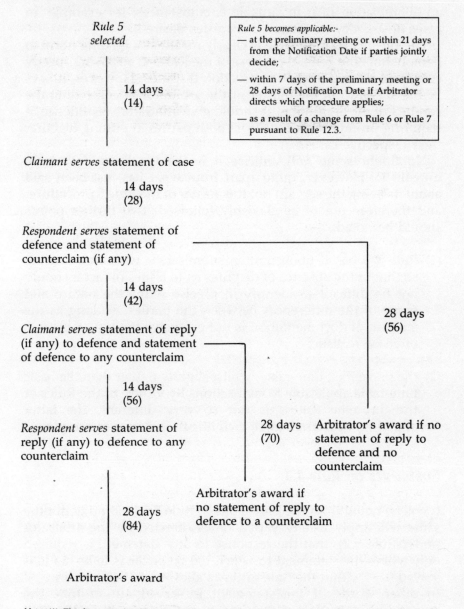

Rule 5
selected

14 days
(14)

Rule 5 becomes applicable:-
— at the preliminary meeting or within 21 days from the Notification Date if parties jointly decide;

— within 7 days of the preliminary meeting or 28 days of Notification Date if Arbitrator directs which procedure applies;

— as a result of a change from Rule 6 or Rule 7 pursuant to Rule 12.3.

Claimant serves statement of case

14 days
(28)

Respondent serves statement of defence and statement of counterclaim (if any)

14 days
(42)

28 days
(56)

Claimant serves statement of reply (if any) to defence and statement of defence to any counterclaim

14 days
(56)

Respondent serves statement of reply (if any) to defence to any counterclaim

28 days
(70)

Arbitrator's award if no statement of reply to defence and no counterclaim

28 days
(84)

Arbitrator's award if no statement of reply to defence to a counterclaim

Arbitrator's award

Note: (1) The figures in brackets are the cumulative number of days from the date when Rule 5 becomes applicable.

(2) Depending upon the number of statements served the period between Rule 5 becoming applicable and the date of the award will range between 56 and 84 days.

The prescribed time-table in Rule 5.3 may not apply as a result of the arbitrator directing otherwise under Rule 5.2. Very often this will be an extension of the prescribed time-table, but may also be an abbreviation of it in suitable circumstances; for example, in cases of urgency or where both parties desire it.

The prescribed time-table is clearly meant as a guiding norm to demonstrate the general purpose of the Rules in achieving speedy economic resolutions of construction disputes. However, it is to be the servant not the master of the arbitrator in controlling the conduct of the arbitration. It should give arbitrators confidence in requiring prompt responses from both parties in putting together their respective cases.

No doubt some will criticise it as being almost invariably unrealistic. However, quite apart from what has just been said about its being the servant not the master of the Rule 5 procedure, and therefore not to be slavishly followed, two further points should be noted:

(1) Rule 5 is based upon written submissions without a hearing so that in the absence of disputes as to issues of fact it should not be difficult to identify in precise terms the nature and scope of the differences between the parties. So long as the amount of documentation is not extensive the time-table will often be realistic;

(2) the prescribed time-table, whilst slightly tighter than the basic time-table applicable to civil actions by virture of the Rules of the Supreme Court, is not so very different, the latter applying, of course, to all civil litigation however complex.

Comments on Rule 5.3

It will be noted from the provisions of Rule 5.3 (and no doubt the same will apply to any varied times directed by the arbitrator under Rule 5.2), that the response to any statement is required only where the statement to which the response is to be made is served '. . . within the time or times allowed by these Rules . . .' In other words, if the statement is served out of time the responding party is not required to respond at all and cannot waive the defaulting party's non-compliance. It will be recalled, of course, that by virtue of Rule 2.7 the parties cannot grant indulgences in respect of time to one another without the express written concurrence of the arbitrator. If one party is fearful of missing the prescribed time, he would be well advised to apply to the arbitrator for an extension of time in accordance with Rule 5.7 *before* the time limit expires, even though before that application is determined he will be serving the statement. If a statement is served in these circumstances, the receiving party would be well advised to prepare the statement in response promptly on the basis that a short extension of time may well be in the event granted by the arbitrator.

Rule 5.4 is also relevant here. This in effect entitles a party to an extension of time of seven days from the date when the arbitrator, under that Rule, notifies the party that unless he receives the statement within seven days of the notification he will proceed on the basis that that party will not be serving the statement in question. If therefore the statement is served within the seven day period it must be allowed. In such case it is submitted that the responding party's time for response operates from the date of the belated service, on the basis that though there has been a default, the Rules *allow* for this to happen with no adverse consequences. It is clearly important that the arbitrator acts promptly under Rule 5.4 where the statement is not served within the original time scale. To the extent that the arbitrator fails to notify under Rule 5.4, it operates as a general extension of time in favour of the defaulting party, leaving the party not in default powerless under the Rules, though the aggrieved party may, as a last resort, apply to the High Court for the removal of the arbitrator under section 13(3) of the 1950 Act.

Rule 5.3 provides that statements of reply to a defence to the claim, or to a defence to any counter-claim, *may* be served. A reply may, of course, not be necessary. However, as under Rule 5 there is to be no hearing, and therefore no opening and closing submissions to the arbitrator, it will very often be appropriate for a reply to be served. Indeed it could often be that a response to the reply would also be desirable so that each party has two bites of the cherry. Perhaps, in the case of the Rule 5 procedure, the Rules should have expressly countenanced this possibility. As it is, this can only be done by a further general direction of the arbitrator. It may be that the arbitrator will consider this possibility at the preliminary meeting so that it can be built in and added to the time-table prescribed under Rule 5.3 or directed under Rule 5.2.

Previously delivered statements

By Rule 5.6 where a party has previously delivered to the arbitrator any statement which satisfies the requirements of Rules 3.4, 3.5 and 5.3.6, the arbitrator may direct that such a statement stands in place of any statement which would otherwise be required to be served under Rule 5.3. This will be useful in a number of situations, for example, where a claimant is keen to get on and so delivers his statement of case at, or before, the preliminary meeting, or where there is a change from the Rule 6 procedure to Rule 5 procedure pursuant to Rule 12.3.

Extensions of time

Rule 5.7 allows a party to apply for an extension of the time prescribed in Rule 5.3 or directed under Rule 5.2. However, its limits must be carefully noted by the parties and by the arbitrator. The granting of an extension of the time required for service is subject to the following:

(1) The application, which must be in writing, must be served on the arbitrator *before* the time limit expires. A copy should be served simultaneously upon the other party.

(2) The arbitrator has a discretion whether to extend time, but before he can even exercise that discretion he must be satisfied that the reason for the application is in respect of matters which could reasonably be considered to be outside the control of the applicant. What is outside the control of the applicant is, of course, a debatable point. Clearly the tighter the time-table the more likely it is that a short temporary difficulty will nevertheless suffice to support a successful application. For example, a three-day bout of 'flu on the part of a party or his representative could be crucial to the ability to meet a 14-day deadline.

(3) The respondent to the application may, of course, consent, in which case the arbitrator can if he wishes give his written concurrence pursuant to Rule 2.7 even if the delay was within the control of the applicant. This is so even if the arbitrator's written concurrence is sought after the original time limit has expired.

(4) The respondent may, within five days of service upon him of the copy of the application, serve written comments upon the arbitrator with a copy to the applicant, and the arbitrator must take such comments into account in exercising his discretion.

Rule 5.7.1 provides that if the arbitrator exercises his discretion in favour of the applicant he will extend by direction in writing '. . . the times for service required by Rule 5.3 or directed under Rule 5.2 . . .' Does this enable a second or further application to be made in respect of an already extended time limit? Put another way, is the extended time limit directed under Rule 5.7 nevertheless still a time for service required by Rule 5.3 or directed under Rule 5.2? An application to further extend an extension previously directed does not fit very easily into the language of Rule 5.7.1. Further, the same result cannot be readily achieved by a subsequent application to extend the originally fixed time limit, rather than an application to extend the already extended time limit. The requirement for service of the application to be before the expiry of the original time for service must make this course of action inappropriate.

An express power to further extend time would have been a sensible provision. The matter is not helped by the wording of Rule 5.4 (dealt with below) enabling the arbitrator to accept late service of statements in certain circumstances. In these circumstances it may be sensible for the arbitrator, when extending time in the first instance, to be somewhat more generous than he otherwise might be to allow for unforeseen problems and secondly, to point out to the applicant that the Rules do not, or might not, permit further extensions of time to be directed by the arbitrator.

Though Rule 5.7 does not expressly require the arbitrator to notify the parties where he declines to extend time for service of a statement, he must clearly deal with the application made which implicitly requires a decision from him one way or another. Obviously it is sensible where the arbitrator is refusing to accede to the application, to so direct in the form of a prompt written direction confirming the original time-table.

Non-compliance with the time-table

Non-compliance with the prescribed or directed time-table and its consequences is dealt with in Rules 5.4 and 5.5.

The consequences of non-compliance, as will be seen below, can be devastating. However, the parties are allowed one non-compliance with impunity in respect of every statement in that the arbitrator has in effect to give a warning notice before proceeding further. The procedure is as follows:

(1) A party fails to serve a statement within the relevant time prescribed by Rule 5.3 or directed under Rule 5.2 (query the position where there has been a failure to comply with the direction under Rule 5.7 extending such time). The statements referred to include the optional statements of reply to defence and reply to defence to counter-claim. Non-compliance may not therefore be a default at all, but simply a decision not to serve a statement in reply.

(2) The arbitrator notifies both parties that he proposes to proceed on the basis that the non-complying party will not be serving the statement unless, within seven days of service of the arbitrator's notification, the statement is served. It is to be noted here that while the arbitrator must notify, there is no time prescribed for this, so that if the arbitrator remains inactive this Rule operates effectively as a general extension of time in favour of the defaulting party. It is up to arbitrators therefore not to let this happen. It does not appear that the arbitrator's notification need be in writing unless the requirement to *serve* the notification, coupled with the operation of Rule 3.2, is implicity recognition of the requirement for a written notice. In any event, the matter is so serious that the arbitrator really must notify in writing.

(3) If the statement is received (query *served* – surely what is meant here is service including deemed service – see Rule 3.3 – not actual receipt, for example, where the statement is lost in the post) within seven days of the date of service of the notification the arbitrator must treat it as effective. If the statement is not received within the seven days the arbitrator must proceed with the reference on the basis that the statement is not going to be served.

(4) If the statement is subsequently served it is to be of no effect unless the arbitrator is satisfied that there was a good and proper reason why:

(i) an application was not made to extend time under Rule 5.7.1 and;

(ii) a statement was not served within the seven day warning period under Rule 5.4.

If the arbitrator is satisfied as to these matters then he must accept the statement as valid. There must, it is submitted, be a limit to the operation of this saving provision for statements served subsequent to the expiry of the seven day warning. To begin with, if, in the absence of the statement, the arbitrator has proceeded to make an award he is *functus officio* and has no power to then re-open or revoke the award. The greatest problem will arise where the statement is served very late in the day. While a party can sometimes be compensated in terms of an order against the defaulting party for costs thrown away, perhaps on an indemnity basis, this may be inadequate compensation if it occurs at a very late stage, for example, as the arbitrator is considering his award. In such circumstances, a court of law might well refuse to allow a pleading even to be amended (if it raised new issues) let alone be served for the first time. Justice might therefore require that the statement be treated as of no effect even if the arbitrator is satisified as to the above matters regarding the failure to serve it earlier. However, it is arguable that the last sentence of Rule 5.4 ties the arbitrators' hands in this respect. It is so worded that provided the arbitrator is satisfied that there was good and proper reason for the failure to serve the statement, it must be treated as effective. While no doubt in cases of extreme late service it will be very difficult for the defaulting party to satisfy the arbitrator on the point of there being a good and proper reason, it is not beyond the realms of possibility that such a situation could arise. Perhaps the Rules ought to have given the arbitrator a real discretion whether to allow the statement in, perhaps in the same way as the court may, but not must, set a judgment aside which has been obtained in the absence of a defence.

A party whose statement is treated as of no effect and who feels aggrieved at the arbitrator's refusal to let it in may, if the arbitrator ought to have been satisfied that there was good and proper reason for late service, apply to the court to have any award set aside under section 23 of the 1950 Act. An alternative may be to seek a declaration from the court, coupled with an interim stay of the arbitration proceedings, that the statement is effective and should be let in.

Non-service of statement of case

If it is the statement of case which is not served, Rule 5.5 requires the arbitrator to make an award dismissing the claim and ordering the claimant to pay the arbitrator's fees and expenses, together with the respondent's costs. Of course, as the claim will not have been dismissed on the merits, the claimant can start a fresh arbitration. Indeed the cost consequences to the claimant of a dismissed claim may be sufficiently insignificant to pursuade a claimant who is unhappy with the appointing body's choice of arbitrator to let the claim be dismissed and to start again with a fresh notice of arbitration. In the High Court a defendant might seek to have any fresh claim stopped in its tracks by an application for it to be struck out as being vexatious or an abuse of the process of the court – see Order 18 Rule 19 of the Rules of the Supreme Court, for example, if a plaintiff was unhappy with the Official Referee to whom a litigation case was assigned. There is no such procedure within these Rules. However, it seems likely that a respondent could go to the court to seek an injunction from the court acting under its inherent jurisdiction to prevent the claimant from proceeding with the second arbitration in appropriate circumstances.

Should the appointing body in such a case appoint the same arbitrator, or would it feel that to do so may result in the appointment of an arbitrator who is not sufficiently independent or impartial because of the history of the matter?

Non-compliance by arbitrator

As the above commentary on Rules 5.4, 5.5 and 5.7 shows, the Rules impose a strict regime in relation to non-compliance by the parties with the time-table prescribed in Rule 5.3 or directed under Rule 5.2.

It is intended that a failure to meet the time-table without good reason should result in a party losing the opportunity to present its case as well, no doubt, as being punished in costs. In these circumstances, can the arbitrator ignore the consequences of non-compliance and permit a statement to be served out of time, by relying upon Rule 12.2 which provides that, subject to the Arbitration Acts 1950 to 1979, any non-compliance by the Arbitrator with the Rules, including those relating to time, shall not of itself affect the validity of an award.

This raises the most difficult questions. It might be argued for instance, that any non-compliance of this kind with the Rules by the arbitrator could amount to misconduct of the proceedings as the arbitrator is flouting the Rules. It is suggested that the only circumstances in which the arbitrator may be able to rely upon Rule 12.2 in such situations is where the statement has been served late, the arbitrator has treated it as valid, and the other party to the arbitration has also treated it as valid and effective without reserving his position in respect of it. If a late statement appears to have been treated as effective by the arbitrator, the party upon whom it is served should raise the matter immediately and seek some resolution on the matter before proceeding further. This may, where the arbitrator, despite objection, treats the statement as valid and effective, require an application to the court for a declaration or for the removal of the arbitrator. A possible alternative is for the aggrieved party to reserve his position expressly in writing to the arbitrator and to the other party in terms that he does not waive the irregularity and, should he so decide following the publication of an award, he may seek to challenge the validity of the award in the courts.

Statements and supporting documents

Rule 5.3.6 provides that a party's statement shall include a list of any documents which that party considers necessary to support any part of the statement together with a copy of the documents in question with any relevant parts upon which reliance is being placed clearly identified.

This method of formulating and identifying the issues, being distinctly unlike traditional pleadings, and its implications on the issue of discovery and inspection of documents has been discussed earlier – see page 43.

It will be remembered – Rule 3.4 – that the statement is to set out the factual and legal basis relied upon. The Rule 5 procedure is not suitable where there is any serious dispute as to relevant facts so that the documents in support are likely to be fairly limited. To the extent, therefore, that any factual contentions in the statements are not disputed, documentary support will not be necessary in terms of evidence. However, if the issue in dispute is, say, the correct interpretation of the wording of a specification, then clearly a copy of the relevant part of the specification will be required.

Under the Rule 5 procedure, many of the disputes will concern the application of the contract conditions or contract documents to an agreed set of facts, involving questions of interpretation and law. It is highly likely therefore that the documents relied on will not only include such things as extracts from the contract documents, architect's instructions, supplier's literature, test results, codes of practice, technical publications, etc., but also on occasions extracts from legal cases and legal textbooks.

Rule 5.3 requires, and it is particularly appropriate in written submissions, that relevant or particularly relevant parts of documents included with the statement are marked up in some way – scoring in the margin in double lines is probably more satisfactory than underlining.

Clearly the statements should be as lucid and concise as possible. This is often easier said than done. To try and achieve this there is no substitute for getting to know in detail the real issues between the parties. To make the best use of the procedure some goodwill between the parties or their representatives is highly desirable so that they can discuss the issues informally, even if without prejudice, before pen is put to paper. This can save much wasted time and effort as well as paper.

Not only must the draftsman of the statement have fully acquainted himself with the issues, he must be clear in his own mind of the points he wishes to make and what documentation he will be using to support his submission. The statement should also, so far as practicable, specify the remedy sought, for example, declaration, damages and so on – see Rule 3.5.

As there is no oral submission or written opening or closing addresses, it may be that the statements, where Rule 5 applies, will be more comprehensive than where Rule 6 (full procedure with a hearing) applies as in the latter case oral or written addresses including, of course, legal argument, will follow later on, though wherever possible they should nevertheless be included in outline in the appropriate statement. Some specimen statements are contained in Appendix 3 to this book.

Clarification of listed documents or further documentation

Rule 5.8 provides that where the arbitrator considers that any of the documents included with any statement requires further clarification by an interview with the parties or otherwise, or that some further document is essential for the arbitrator to properly arrive at a decision, he may require such clarification or further document by notice in writing.

If it is clarification by interview which is required by the arbitrator, such clarification is to be obtained in accordance with the arbitrator's directions. This applies also to any other form of clarification. Clearly, the arbitrator needs to be careful to comply with the rules of natural justice and should not deal with a party unilaterally. Any interview should take place in the presence of all parties or they should at least be given ample opportunity to both be present and to put their views.

If a further document is required, it is to be supplied to the arbitrator with a copy to the other party. Compliance with the arbitrator's notice requiring a further document is to be forthwith.

The Rules do not provide expressly for what is to happen in the event of non-compliance with the arbitrator's notice or direction under Rule 5.8. Where it causes no injustice to the other party the arbitrator can proceed in the absence of the clarification or further document. Otherwise, there is as a last resort the possibility of seeking the assistance of the High Court by means of a direction under section 12(6)(b) or (d) of the 1950 Act, or the enhancement of the arbitrator's powers under section 5 of the 1979 Act.

In practice, the use by the arbitrator of this Rule will as often be at the behest of the one of the parties as of the arbitrator's own motion.

Rule 5.8 does not include a power for the arbitrator to seek clarification of any statement itself but only a document listed in a statement. This is surprising as it would have been sensible to include a power for clarification of anything included in the statement. It may be an accidental omission from the Rules in which case it may be included in any subsequent amendment of them. If it is a party rather than the arbitrator who is seeking clarification of something contained in a statement, it is always possible for that party to apply to the arbitrator for the other party from whom clarification is sought to provide further and better particulars of the statement and the arbitrator can so direct if he accedes to the application.

The award

Rule 5.9 deals with the award. The arbitrator must, subject to Rule 5.9.2, publish his award within 28 days after, whichever is the earlier of the following:

● receipt of the last of the statements and documents referred to in Rule 5.3; or

● where a statement has not been served, the expiry of the last of the times allowed by the Rules for its service.

The reference in Rule 5.9.1 to Rule 5.3 is clearly only a reference to the statements of case, defence, counter-claim and reply rather than to the time-table prescribed for their service. Thus if the time for service is extended under Rule 5.7, or enlarged under Rule 5.4, the time limit applies subject thereto.

Where there has been a clarification of a document or further documents supplied in accordance with Rule 5.8, Rule 5.9.1 does not appear automatically to extend the 28 day period, so that strictly speaking the arbitrator must rely on Rule 5.9.2.

Under Rule 5.9.2 the arbitrator may decide to publish his award later than the 28 day period referred to in Rule 5.9.1 and, if so, he must *before* the expiry of the 28 days, immediately notify the parties in writing when his award will be published.

If the parties are not to have an award within 28 days it is clearly right that the arbitrator should, as soon as he has decided that he will not meet the 28 day limit, notify the parties so that they know where they stand.

The arbitrator may reach his decision not to publish his award within 28 days even before that period starts to run; for example, where he knows that he will be seeking technical or legal advice which will cause him to overrun the period.

If he does seek technical or legal advice, he should disclose the nature of this to the parties and allow them to make a further written submission dealing with it.

If, without notifying the parties, the arbitrator actually takes longer than the 28 day period to publish his award it cannot be challenged on the grounds of his not having complied with Rule 5.9.2 – see Rule 12.2. However, if the delay is unreasonable, the arbitrator can be removed by the High Court under section 13(3) of the 1950 Act in which event the arbitrator would lose his entitlement to receive any remuneration in respect of his services.

For some brief comments in relation to awards generally reference should be made to the earlier commentary on Rule 11 – see page 60 *et seq.*

Chapter 6

Full procedure with a hearing – Rule 6

Introduction

Rule 6 provides for an arbitration with a hearing. As such it is suited to disputes where there are issues of fact which cannot be agreed and which will therefore require the examination and cross-examination of witnesses of fact. Furthermore, an oral hearing is also appropriate where experts disagree, again to enable examination and cross-examination to take place so that the arbitrator can reach a conclusion based upon the evidence before him.

There may also be occasions where the dispute, though possible to resolve using written submissions (for example, the interpretation of a specification or a question of legal argument) could usefully benefit from oral debate. However, while this can often be very effective in testing the issues it is likely to be the most expensive way of proceeding, certainly if lawyers are used. Either the arbitrator would have to be sure that this was the best practical way of resolving the dispute or both parties would have to require it before the arbitrator should so order.

Even though Rule 6 provides for a hearing, it need not be all orally conducted. Written opening and closing addresses may well be convenient and economical. In addition, the early exchange of proofs of evidence and experts' reports may drastically reduce the need for detailed, sometimes laborious, examination and cross-examination of witnesses. Arbitrators should use every endeavour to narrow issues as far as possible before the hearing rather than to let everything rest on the hearing itself. Doing so may well lead to settlement of the arbitration and, if not, it should reduce significantly the length and cost of the hearing itself.

There can be little doubt that many of the major construction industry arbitrations which take place will require an oral hearing in some form or another. Even here it may be possible to separate out issues for written submissions or for sub-hearings and again this may lead to settlement and/or a saving in time and cost.

Sometimes the Rule 6 procedure with its hearing will be required by the arbitrator under Rule 12.3 where it appears to be necessary for the just and expeditious determination to change from another Rule, often Rule 5 (procedure without a hearing) – for example, where it appears part way through the Rule 5 procedure that there are disputes as to relevant fact. As mentioned in Chapter 4 – see page 84 – in many disputes it will be highly convenient to allot various issues to various Rules for their resolution. The Rules do not appear to expressly countenance this possibility, though the arbitrator should seek to get the parties to agree to this whenever it appears to him to be appropriate. Taking into account that often Rule 6 will apply where the issues are many and complex, coupled with the general requirement for statements of case, as opposed to traditional pleadings, the arbitrator will frequently direct a longer time scale under Rule 6.2 than that prescribed in Rule 6.3. In addition, Rule 6.2 enables the arbitrator to direct that an alternative procedure to that of statements of case, etc., should apply, for example, traditional pleadings. This aspect of Rule 6.2 is commented upon further – see page 116.

Rule 6

6.1　Rule 6 applies to the conduct of the arbitration where:

> **.1**　the parties have so decided under Rule 4.2.1; or

> **.2**　the provisions of Rule 4.3.1 have come into effect and the Arbitrator has directed that Rule 6 shall apply.

6.2　Rule 6.3 shall apply except to the extent that the Arbitrator otherwise directs or, subject to Rule 2.7, the parties otherwise agree.

6.3　**.1**　The Claimant shall, within 28 days after the date when Rule 6 becomes applicable, serve a statement of case.

> **.2**　If the Claimant serves a statement of case within the time or times allowed by these Rules the Respondent shall, within 28 days after service of the Claimant's statement of case, serve

a statement of defence to the Claimant's statement of case; and

a statement of any counterclaim.

.3 If the Respondent serves a statement of defence within the time or times allowed by these Rules the Claimant may, within 14 days after such service, serve a statement of reply to the defence.

.4 If the Respondent serves a statement of counterclaim within the time or times allowed by these Rules the Claimant shall, within 28 days after such service, serve a statement of defence to the Respondent's counterclaim.

.5 If the Claimant serves a statement of defence to the Respondent's statement of counterclaim within the time or times allowed by these Rules the Respondent may, within 14 days after such service, serve a statement of reply to the defence.

.6 The Claimant with

his statement of case and

any statement setting out a reply to the Respondent's statement of defence and

his statement of defence to any statement of counterclaim by the Respondent

and the Respondent with

his statement of defence and

any statement of counterclaim and

any statement setting out a reply to the Claimant's statement of defence to any counterclaim

shall include a list of any documents the Claimant or Respondent as the case may be considers necessary to support any part of the relevant statement and a copy of the principal documents on which reliance will be placed identifying clearly in each document the relevant part or parts on which reliance will be placed.

6.4 If a party does not serve a statement of

case, defence, reply to the defence, counterclaim, defence to the counterclaim or reply to the defence to the counterclaim within the relevant time required by Rule 6.3 or directed or agreed under Rule 6.2 the Arbitrator shall notify the parties that he proposes to proceed on the basis that the party will not be serving the same unless within 7 days of the date of service of that notification the relevant statement is served. If within 7 days of the date of service of that notification the relevant statement is not received the Arbitrator shall proceed on the basis that the party will not be serving the same. If the relevant statement is subsequently served it shall be of no effect unless the Arbitrator is satisfied that there was a good and proper reason both why an application was not made within the time required by Rule 6.7.1 and why a statement was not served within 7 days of his notice given under Rule 6.4.

6.5   If the Claimant either does not serve his statement of case within the time or times allowed by these Rules or if served it is of no effect by reason of Rule 6.4 the Arbitrator shall make an award dismissing the claim and ordering the Claimant to pay the Arbitrator's fees and expenses and any costs hitherto incurred by the Respondent.

6.6   Provided that where the party has, or the parties have, previously delivered to the Arbitrator a statement or statements setting out the matter or matters in dispute including the factual and legal basis relied upon together with the information where relevant required by Rule 3.5 and a list of any documents and a copy of the principal documents as required by Rule 6.3.6, the Arbitrator may direct that such statement or statements shall stand in place of all or any of the statements or documents to be delivered in compliance with Rule 6.3.

6.7   .1   Subject to a written application by the Claimant or Respondent for an extension of times for service required by Rule 6.3 or directed or agreed under Rule 6.2 being served upon the Arbitrator before the expiry of the relevant time for service, the Arbitrator may in his discretion extend by direction in writing to the Claimant and the Respondent the times for service required by Rule 6.3 or directed or agreed under Rule 6.2.

.2   A copy of any written application under Rule 6.7.1 shall be served upon the other party who may, within 5 days of such service, serve written comments thereon upon the Arbitrator and serve a copy thereof upon the applicant. In exercising his discretion under Rule 6.7.1 the Arbitrator shall take such written comments into account.

6.8   The Arbitrator shall, after receipt of the last of the statements and documents referred to in Rule 6.3 or after the expiry of the last of the times allowed by these Rules for their service, whichever is the earlier, after consultation with the parties, notify the parties in writing of the date(s) when and the place where the oral hearing will be held. The Arbitrator shall immediately notify the parties in writing of any change in such date(s) or place.

6.9 **.1** The Arbitrator shall publish his award within 28 days of the close of the hearing.

    .2 The Arbitrator may decide to publish his award later than the expiry of the aforementioned 28 day period and if so he shall, prior to the expiry thereof, immediately notify the parties in writing when his award will be published.

Selecting Rule 6

Rule 6 applies to the conduct of the arbitration where either:

● The parties have jointly selected it under Rule 4.2.1; or

● The parties have not been able to agree any of the procedures in Rules 5, 6 or 7 for the conduct of the arbitration so that the provisions of Rule 4.3.1. have come into effect and the arbitrator has, having regard to any information supplied by and/or any representations made by the parties, directed that Rule 6 shall apply;

● The arbitrator has switched procedure to Rule 6 from Rule 5 or Rule 7 pursuant to Rule 12.3.

Where the parties jointly decide upon Rule 6 they do so either at the preliminary meeting or, if no preliminary meeting is to be held, within 21 days from the Notification Date – Rule 4.1.
If the parties have not agreed to select Rule 6 then the Arbitrator, if he intends to direct that Rule 6 shall apply, must so direct either not less than seven days after the preliminary meeting, or if no preliminary meeting is to be held, within 28 days of the Notification Date.

When does Rule 6 become applicable?

The Rule 6.3 time-table operates from the date when Rule 6 becomes applicable which can be calculated in the same manner as for the time-table under Rule 5.3 – see page 97.

Time-table for Rule 6 procedure

A table setting out the time-table under Rule 6.3 from the period when Rule 6 becomes applicable is set out at page 117.

Rule 6.3 prescribes a time-table for the service of statements of case, defence, reply to defence, counterclaim, defence to counterclaim and reply to defence to counterclaim. The arbitrator may, under Rule 6.2, direct a different time-table; alternatively the parties may agree a different time-table, subject however to the express written concurrence of the arbitrator under Rule 2.7, where the agreement is for the time-table to be extended.

Where the arbitration is at all complex or raises a number of different issues suitable only for the Rule 6 procedure, a time-table other than that prescribed can be expected. Even so it is always useful to have a prescribed time-table as a basis from which to operate the procedure for the service of statements. It is also useful in giving the arbitrator support where he imposes a tight time-table upon the parties, perhaps in the face of strong objection by one of them.

In addition the time-table, whether that prescribed under Rule 6.3 or directed under Rule 6.2, may in certain circumstances be extended by virtue of Rules 6.4 and 6.7.

Comments on Rule 6.2

The wording of Rule 6.2 enables the arbitrator to direct any procedure he wishes quite apart from altering the Rule 6.3 time-table. This could mean a departure from the use of statements of case which is fundamental to the achieving of the main objective of the Rules, namely, as speedy and economical resolution of the dispute as is possible, consistent with the rules of natural justice.

The arbitrator under Rule 6.2 could therefore order traditional pleadings in place of statements of case, etc. It is to be hoped that this will not happen very often. If the arbitrator does depart from the statements of case as described in Rule 3.4, then Rules 6.3, 6.4, 6.5, 6.6, 6.7 and 6.8 appear not to apply and the arbitration will proceed much as it does without these Rules applying, except that Rule 6.9 regarding the publication of the award and any of the rules of general application will where appropriate apply.

It may be that the parties, with or without legal advice, will agree that there should be a departure from statements of case, etc., and that therefore Rules 6.4, 6.5, 6.6, 6.7 and 6.8 should not

Time-table for Rule 6 procedure

Rule 6 maximum prescribed time-table for delivery of statements if no extensions or abbreviations

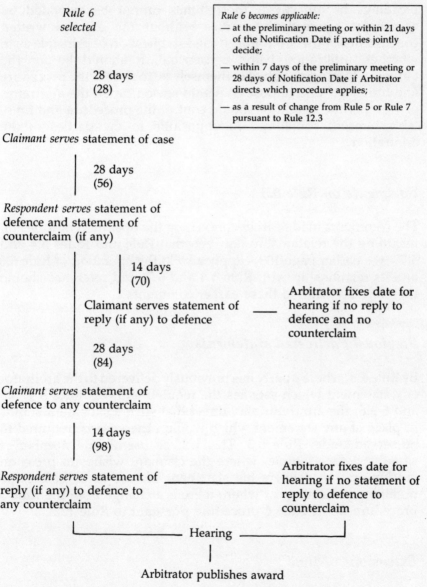

*Rule 6
selected*

28 days
(28)

> *Rule 6 becomes applicable:*
> — at the preliminary meeting or within 21 days of the Notification Date if parties jointly decide;
> — within 7 days of the preliminary meeting or 28 days of Notification Date if Arbitrator directs which procedure applies;
> — as a result of change from Rule 5 or Rule 7 pursuant to Rule 12.3

Claimant serves statement of case

28 days
(56)

Respondent serves statement of defence and statement of counterclaim (if any)

14 days
(70)

Claimant serves statement of reply (if any) to defence ⎯⎯ Arbitrator fixes date for hearing if no reply to defence and no counterclaim

28 days
(84)

Claimant serves statement of defence to any counterclaim

14 days
(98)

Respondent serves statement of reply (if any) to defence to any counterclaim ⎯⎯⎯⎯ Arbitrator fixes date for hearing if no statement of reply to defence to counterclaim

⎣⎯⎯⎯⎯⎯⎯ Hearing ⎯⎯⎯⎯⎯⎯⎦

Arbitrator publishes award

Note: (1) The figures in brackets are the cumulative number of days from the date when Rule 6 becomes applicable.

(2) Depending upon the number of statements served the period between Rule 6 becoming applicable and the closing date for service of statements will range between 70 and 98 days.

apply. At the end of the day there is probably little the arbitrator can do in relation to this except to seek to establish that it is the genuine intention of the parties to do this. Even if it is done, this does not affect the operation of Rule 2.7, whereby once any time-table is directed, whether in respect of service of traditional pleadings or otherwise, those times cannot be extended by agreement between the parties without the express written concurrence of the arbitrator. It raises a question of principle as to whether, arbitration being consensual, it should be for the parties, if they agree between themselves, to choose the procedure and time-table and impose it, within reason, upon the arbitrator; or whether the arbitrator should control the procedure and time-table himself, sometimes in opposition to the parties in the arbitration.

Comments on Rule 6.3

The comments made earlier concerning the operation of Rule 5.3, including the relationship between that Rule and Rules 5.4 and 5.7 – see earlier page 100 – apply also to the operation of Rule 6.3 and its relationship with Rule 6.4 and 6.7, and reference should therefore be made to these earlier comments.

Previously delivered statements

By Rule 6.6, where a party has previously delivered to the arbitrator any statement which satisfies the requirements of Rules 3.4, 3.5 and 6.3.6, the arbitrator may direct that such a statement stands in place of any statement which would otherwise be required to be served under Rule 6.3. This will be useful in a number of situations, for example, where the claimant wishes to press on quickly and so delivers his statement of case at or before the preliminary meeting, or where there is a change from the Rule 5 procedure to the Rule 6 procedure pursuant to Rule 12.3.

Extensions of time

Rule 6.7 allows a party to apply for an extension of the time prescribed in Rule 6.3 or directed or agreed under Rule 6.2 subject, however, to compliance with the requirements of the Rule. The comments made earlier on the application of Rule 5.7 – page 102 – relating to such matters as the timing of the application and the possible difficulty of repeat applications are applicable here also.

However, a major difference between Rule 5.7 and Rule 6.7 is that the latter rule, unlike the former, does not require the arbitrator to be satisfied that the reason for the application is in respect of matters which could reasonably be considered to be outside the control of the applicant. Provided, therefore, the application is in writing and served upon the arbitrator before the expiry of the relevant time limit, the arbitrator has a considerable discretion in extending time. Even so the arbitrator should constantly keep in mind the need to keep delays to a minimum.

Non-compliance with the time-table

Non-compliance with the prescribed, directed or agreed time-table and its consequences is dealt with in Rule 6.4 and Rule 6.5.

The earlier comments on the operation of Rule 5.4 and 5.5 apply equally here also – page 103. It is to be noted that in the last line of Rule 5.4 it refers to the service of the arbitrator's notice given under that Rule, whereas in the last line of Rule 6.4 it does not refer to the arbitrator's notice having been served. This appears to have been an unintentional omission and it is suggested it should be treated as of no real consequence.

Statements and supporting documents

Rule 6.3.6 provides that a party's statement shall include a list of any documents which that party considers necessary to support any part of the statement, together with a copy of the principal documents on which reliance will be placed and with any relevant part clearly identified. Many of the comments made earlier about Rule 5.3 – page 108 – concerning the need to understand the issues, and for statements to be lucid and concise, apply equally to Rule 6.3.

The following further points are of particular relevance to Rule 6.3.

Only the principal documents relied upon will accompany the statement. In order to be able at such an early stage in the reference to identify the principally relevant documents, a very firm grasp of the issues and objectives is needed. Even here there may be difficulty, for it is not always clear what are the major issues in dispute until after all statements have been served. The arbitrator should at the preliminary meeting seek to identify areas of agreement and disagreement between the parties. In order to do this the parties or their representatives should firstly be fully briefed before the preliminary meeting, and secondly, be ready and willing to co-operate in the process of narrowing the issues so that the documentation as a whole can be kept to a minimum and the principal documents more readily identified.

Where, as is likely to be the case where the Rule 6 procedure applies, there is considerable dispute as to the facts, there is also likely to be a considerable number of relevant documents in the lists which accompanies the statements. After all statements have been served it may well be possible by a careful consideration of the statements and the parties' principal documents to agree just which of the documents in the list will be needed to be inserted into trial bundles for use at the hearing.

The parties are also reminded of the provisions of Rule 3.4 and Rule 3.5 in the preparation of statements – see page 43.

As there will be an oral hearing under the Rule 6 procedure, there is every reason to believe that the statements will not need to deal in so much detail with matters which might otherwise be in an opening address or other submission made by the parties or their representatives at the hearing, whether oral or in writing. Accordingly, the statements may well be shorter than they would be where Rule 5 (procedure without a hearing) is selected for the conduct of the arbitration.

Though there is to be an oral hearing it may be possible to limit its scope essentially to disputed evidence of fact or expert opinion, by the prior exchange of proofs of evidence and experts' reports, and also by a meeting of experts. In some circumstances it may even be possible to append proofs of evidence and experts' reports to statements which could save considerable time later.

The Rule 6 procedure will be appropriate not only where there is a dispute as to relevant facts, but also where the expert opinion evidence of the parties is at variance and requires testing by oral cross-examination of the expert witnesses.

Unlike the position where Rule 5 (procedure without a hearing) is selected for the conduct of the arbitration with written submissions only, there is no equivalent to Rule 5.8 which expressly enables the arbitrator to seek clarification of listed documents by interview or to call for further documents which he considers essential in order to properly decide on the matters in dispute. This is perhaps a surprising omission, as such clarification or further documents will obviously be relevant on occasions for the proper and comprehensive preparation for an oral hearing or any written submissions associated with it. Despite the absence of such an express power the arbitrator can of his own motion, or upon application of a party, require clarification or further documents under his general authority to control the reference by whatever fair and reasonable procedures, not in conflict with the Rules, he may choose to adopt. In addition, so far as further documentation is concerned, the arbitrator has express power under Rule 12.1.7 to order a party to produce documents.

Fixing the hearing date

By virtue of Rule 6.8, the arbitrator must, after receipt of the last statement and documents referred to in Rule 5.3, or after the last of the times allowed by the Rules for their service, whichever is earlier, and after consultation with the parties, notify the parties in writing of the date and place of hearing. If the date or place is subsequently changed the arbitrator shall again notify the parties in writing.

In practice, it may well be that on many occasions the hearing date has already been fixed even as early as the preliminary meeting. The fixing of a hearing date early on in the procedure has the benefit of concentrating the minds of the parties or their representatives and often acts as a spur to meet the time-table leading up to the hearing.

There is no time limit stated in Rule 6.8 as to when the arbitrator must proceed to fix a date and place or as to how long in advance that date is to be fixed, though the general tenor of Rule 6.8 suggests that it should be fixed promptly. However, the nature of disputes for which the Rule 6 procedure is suitable will vary considerably. After service of all of the statements there may well still be much to be done in complying with directions given in relation to such matters as:

● experts reports,

● meeting of experts,

● preparation and exchange of proofs of evidence of witnesses of fact,

● agreement of plans, photographs or other documents,

● preparation of trial bundles.

Rule 6.8 refers to consultation by the arbitrator with the parties. This might well take place at a pre-trial review after all or most of the directions have been complied with. Its purpose will be to reconsider all of the outstanding issues which may then have been narrowed and clarified, with a view to how best to arrange the hearing, for example, perhaps in the form of sub-trials or even a preliminary issue, and also such matters as written opening addresses, estimates of the length of the oral hearing and so on. It may also be possible even at this stage to switch to Rule 5 (procedure without a hearing) if it turns out that the parties have agreed the facts and if any experts appointed agree in their opinions.

It is not unusual in construction cases coming before the courts as official referees' business for a hearing date, with at least a provisional assessment of its likely length, to be given at the first general directions hearing, particularly if the hearing is not expected to be a long one. This gives purpose to the time-table and also ensures that the case will not simply go to sleep due to inactivity. However, provided the arbitrator is prepared to properly apply the Rules as to time for service of statements, etc., and to keep a close eye on compliance with other directions there should be no risk of this occurring even without a hearing date fixed from an early stage.

The award

Under Rule 6.9.1 the arbitrator must, subject to Rule 6.9.2 publish his award within 28 days of the close of the hearing. Under Rule 6.9.2 if the arbitrator decides to publish his award later than the expiry of the 28 day period, he must, before the expiry of that period, immediately notify the parties in writing of when his award will be published. Arbitrators should endeavour wherever possible to publish the award within the 28 day period. On occasions this may not be possible. Sometimes the arbitrator may appreciate this at the close of the formal hearing, for example, where there is much documentation and evidence to review, or where there is to be a written closing address sometime after the oral hearing has finished.

However if the arbitrator delays unreasonably in publishing the award he can be removed by the High Court under section 13(3) of the 1950 Act in which event the arbitrator would not be entitled to receive any remuneration in respect of his services.

For some brief comments in relation to awards generally reference should be made to the earlier commentary on Rule 11 – see page 60.

Chapter 7

Short procedure with a hearing – Rule 7

Introduction

Rule 7 provides for arbitration in a short form with an oral hearing. The procedure for the conduct of the arbitration under Rule 7 has very little in common with the procedures under Rule 5 (procedure without a hearing) or Rule 6 (full procedure with a hearing).

Under Rule 7 there are no formal statements of case and no witnesses. The oral hearing is simply for the parties briefly to put their cases to the arbitrator.

The short procedure is suitable where a quick award is both required and practicable, being especially suitable for disputes requiring resolution during the running of the contract where the decision of the arbitrator is likely to have an important bearing upon the way in which the contract continues to run, for example, whether the specified loading requirements for piles have been met.

Rule 7 may also be suitable for obtaining decisions on disputes even where there is no great sense of urgency, but where the dispute lends itself to the informality of the Rule 7 procedure, for example, whether two sections of mortar work on a brick facade are an acceptable colour match. Such a dispute may be able to be readily resolved by an inspection and a short oral submission by each of the parties to the arbitrator.

If there is a dispute as to relevant facts or disputed experts' opinions Rule 6 (full procedure with a hearing) will be applicable. Even if there is no such dispute, if there is a significant amount of documentation, Rule 5 (procedure without a hearing) may be more appropriate.

Whether the Rule 7 procedure is suitable or not will often depend upon the particular dispute rather than on any classification into which the dispute falls. For example, it could be that there is a dispute concerning the architect's unwillingness to issue a certificate of making good defects. Such a dispute may be straightforward and easily resolved by the arbitrator, for example, whether the paintwork is of an adequate standard so that it should be acceptable under the contract and not regarded as a defect. Alternatively, the dispute could raise major complicated issues, for example, the architect contending that there is a serious failure on the part of the contractor in respect of workmanship relating to the discovery of a defective pile, with the contractor contending that it is a defect in the pile design for which he is not responsible.

As will be seen from the detailed discussion of the operation of Rule 7 which follows, it opens the way for very prompt and inexpensively obtained binding awards in appropriate circumstances.

If Rule 7 is to be selected, this must be by agreement between the parties, the arbitrator cannot impose the Rule 7 procedure on the parties.

Where the Rule 7 procedure applies to the conduct of the arbitration, each side will generally bear its own costs though there is an exception which is discussed later.

Rule 7

7.1 **.1** Rule 7 applies to the conduct of the arbitration where parties have so decided under Rule 4.2.2.

  .2 Each party shall bear his own costs unless for special reasons the Arbitrator at his discretion otherwise directs.

7.2 Within 21 days of the date when Rule 7 has become applicable the hearing shall be held at such place and on such day and at such time as the Arbitrator shall direct. No evidence except the documents referred to in Rule 7.3 may be adduced at the hearing except as the Arbitrator may otherwise direct or allow.

7.3 **.1** Not later than 7 days before the hearing documents necessary to support the oral submissions and the relevant part or parts thereof shall be identified to the other party and a copy of any such document not in the possession of the other party shall be served upon that party.

  .2 A copy of the documents referred to in Rule 7.3.1 shall be served upon the Arbitrator 7 days before the hearing and shall be available at the hearing.

7.4   The Arbitrator may direct that such procedures shall be followed at the hearing and such documents made available as he considers necessary for the just and expeditious determination of the dispute.

7.5   At the end of the hearing the Arbitrator shall

either   thereupon make his award and if made orally shall forthwith confirm his award in writing

or   publish his award within 7 days of the hearing.

The Arbitrator may decide to publish his award later than the expiry of the aforementioned 7 day period and if so, he shall, prior to the expiry thereof, immediately notify the parties in writing when his award will be published.

Selecting Rule 7 – and the preliminary meeting

Rule 7 applies to the conduct of the arbitration where the parties have so decided under Rules 4.2.1 and 4.2.2. In the absence of a joint decision by the parties, the arbitrator will select either Rule 5 (procedure without a hearing) or Rule 6 (full procedure with a hearing) in accordance with Rule 4.3.1.

By virtue of Rule 4.2.1 and Rule 4.2.2, if Rule 7 is to apply the parties must jointly so decide at the preliminary meeting. By virtue of the words in Rule 4.2.1 '. . . subject to Rule 4.2.2 . . .', there must be a preliminary meeting before Rule 7 can apply.

By Rule 4.2.2, if the claimant wishes Rule 7 to apply, he must within a reasonable time after the commencement of the arbitration and '. . . at least 7 days before a decision under Rule 4.2.1 is required . . .' formulate his case in writing in sufficient detail to identify the matters in dispute. This time limit for formulation of the case in writing is a strange method by which to indicate the time-table. It at least appears to raise the possibility that a preliminary meeting may not always be necessary where Rule 7 is selected, and yet a reading of Rules 4.2.1 and 4.2.2 as a whole seems to indicate that a preliminary meeting must always be held as the joint decision, which is required for the Rule 7 procedure to apply, must be made at the preliminary meeting. The reference, therefore, to a date seven days before a decision under Rule 4.2.1 is required is in fact a reference to seven days before the preliminary meeting takes place. It would have been much easier for the Rules to simply say so. This date will generally be at most no later than 14 days after the Notification Date, unless the preliminary meeting is postponed under Rule 4.1.

The written case which has been formulated must be submitted to the respondent with a copy to the arbitrator. Rule 4.2.2 then goes on to state that at the time of submitting the written case the claimant must state that at the preliminary meeting he will request the respondent to agree to Rule 7. It would be sensible for the arbitrator, when confirming the Notification Date to the parties, which he should invariably do, to also remind them of the above requirements if Rule 7 is to apply, and to ask for a copy of the claimant's statement to the respondent that at the preliminary meeting he will be requesting the respondent to agree to Rule 7.

If at the time of the preliminary meeting, it appears that there have been any irregularities in the requirements which have to be fulfilled prior to the preliminary meeting, no doubt, as the operation of Rule 7 depends upon agreement between the parties in any event, any such irregularities can be waived if appropriate.

The requirement for a written case to be formulated prior to the preliminary meeting and prior, therefore, to the joint decision that Rule 7 is to apply is clearly a necessary requirement, so that the arbitrator can form a view which he can discuss with the parties as to whether the dispute is amenable to the Rule 7 procedure. If it is, then the written formulation of the case will replace the need for any formal statement of case.

As stated above, the effect of Rule 4.2 appears to be that if the Rule 7 procedure is to apply to the conduct of the arbitration a preliminary meeting must be held at which the decision will be made, whereas the Rule 5 and Rule 6 procedures can be selected jointly by the parties even without a preliminary meeting.

It may be surmised that the reasoning behind the requirement for a preliminary meeting is to enable the issues in dispute to be considered carefully by the arbitrator to determine whether the Rule 7 procedure is appropriate. There could be a tendency for the parties in their understandable desire to find a quick and inexpensive solution to the dispute, particularly if they are unrepresented, to agree that Rule 7 should apply when it is impracticable – for example, there are disputes of fact or expert technical opinion or the dispute will require for its resolution the consideration of a significant amount of documentation.

The arbitrator should therefore have the opportunity to give the parties the benefit of his views before they finally decide. The arbitrator cannot force his views upon the parties if they decide upon Rule 7 in the face of objection from the arbitrator. However, once Rule 7 has been selected, there seems nothing to stop the arbitrator directing, pursuant to Rule 12.3 that a different Rule, namely Rule 5 (procedure without a hearing) or Rule 6 (full procedure with a hearing) should be used for the conduct of the arbitration and to switch to that Rule accordingly. In these circumstances it would have been sensible to require the arbitrator's consent also to the Rule 7 procedure applying in the first instance.

Once Rule 7 has been jointly agreed at the preliminary meeting, the arbitrator will give any necessary directions.

The written case

The claimant's written case has to be formulated and submitted within a reasonable time of commencement of the arbitration and at least seven days before the preliminary meeting. As to when there is a 'commencement of the arbitration' see earlier comments in Chapter 2 at page 13. The reason for requiring the written case to be formulated and submitted 'within a reasonable time' is puzzling. The reference to ' . . . at least 7 days before a decision under Rule 4.2.1 is required . . .' ensures that the maximum period for this in any event is 14 days from the Notification Date, unless the date of the preliminary meeting is postponed. In practice, the preliminary meeting may well be held within a period considerably less than the 21 days allowed so that the 14 day maximum period is likely to, in practice, be very much less than this. As the 'commencement of the arbitration' for this purpose is probably the date of service of the written notice under the JCT Arbitration Agreement, the reference to 'within a reasonable time' may be directed at the situation where there is some delay in the selection and appointment of the arbitrator both of which must take place before there is a Notification Date from which all the time scales operate – Rule 2.5.

In appropriate circumstances therefore, the formulation of the written case needs to have been completed some considerable time before there is a Notification Date in existence if there has been any delay, for example, between the nomination of an arbitrator by an appointing body and the agreement of the parties to the arbitrator's terms and conditions of engagement. However, even if to satisfy the requirement of formulating the case within a reasonable time of the commencement of the arbitration, it is necessary to prepare a written case before the Notification Date, until the arbitrator has been appointed (synonymous with the Notification Date), there is no method of fulfilling the requirement in Rule 4.2.2 to submit a copy of the written case to the arbitrator.

The formulation of a written case by the claimant can take any number of forms from an elaborate Scotts Schedule dealing with, for example, the 'snagging list', to a letter setting out the points in issue, or even, if adequate, a copy of correspondence between the parties which states the issues in sufficient detail. As, generally speaking, no costs are awarded under this Rule, the written case will more often than not be formulated by non-lawyers, except perhaps where a party has his own in-house lawyer.

There is no provision for the respondent to submit a written response. The main objective of speed would be eroded if a time-table for exchanging statements of case, defence, counterclaim, etc., were to be prescribed.

Though Rule 4.2.2 refers to the written case being submitted to the respondent rather than being served upon him, it is probable that the written case at least qualifies as a *'document'* under Rule 3.1 so that the provisions as to service in Rule 3.2 and 3.3 apply.

It is most important that the claimant submits a sufficiently detailed written case in order, firstly, that there will be no delay which might otherwise be caused by the need for further written details of the case; and secondly, to enable the arbitrator to reach a decision based upon adequate information when the oral hearing takes place.

As the operation of the Rule 7 procedure is by joint decision of the parties, it might often be sensible for the parties to jointly formulate the case itself for decision by the arbitrator, though it should be remembered that the written case should only provide the details of the issues in dispute and will not normally contain the detailed contentions of either party which will be the subject of the oral hearing itself.

Time-table and documentation for Rule 7 procedure

As can be seen from the above commentary on the selection of the Rule 7 procedure, by the time it has been agreed by the parties at the preliminary meeting that Rule 7 shall apply to the conduct of the arbitration, the arbitrator and the respondent will already have received the claimant's written case in sufficient detail to identify the matters in dispute.

Rule 7.2 provides that the oral hearing is then to be held within 21 days of the date when Rule 7 became applicable. This must be the date of the preliminary meeting. As the applicable date can only be the date of the preliminary meeting under Rule 4.2.2, it would have been simpler to say so. Again, the use of such oblique wording might cause confusion by indicating a possibility that the Rule 7 procedure can be selected without the need for a preliminary meeting to take place.

At the preliminary meeting the arbitrator gives any necessary directions which will include the fixing of the place, day and time of the oral hearing to take place within 21 days of the preliminary meeting – see Rule 7.2.

Very often it will be possible to shorten this 21 day period. Indeed so much so that if the parties and the arbitrator agree, the oral hearing can take place immediately after the preliminary meeting. If this is required the parties should ensure that the necessary documents – see Rule 7.3.1 – have been supplied to one another and to the arbitrator in sufficient time.

Documentation

Not later than seven days before the hearing, any documents (for example, the specification, instructions, certificates etc.) necessary to support the oral submissions, together with any relevant part or parts thereof shall be identified to the other party and a copy of any such document not in the possession of the other party shall be served upon that party. A copy of all the documents must also be served upon the arbitrator seven days before the hearing (presumably at least seven days before, rather than exactly seven days before, despite the wording in Rule 7.3.2). Such documents must also be available at the hearing.

If a party fails to comply with the requirements of Rule 7.3 as to the provision of documents, it is submitted that the arbitrator can proceed with the hearing without them. This may lead to a dismissal of the claimant's claim where he has failed to supply them. While the parties are still happy to use the Rule 7 procedure, there should be no problem in any event. If either party wishes to resile from his agreement that the Rule 7 procedure should apply, they should not be allowed effectively to achieve this by failing to supply necessary documents.

The late supply, rather than a complete failure to supply, documents is more difficult. If all parties agree to accept documents late there is no problem. If a party objects to documents introduced late the arbitrator is in some difficulty. It is not at all clear that the arbitrator has power to accept documents served late against a party's wishes. In other words he cannot easily waive the seven day requirement of Rule 7.3. It depends upon whether the seven day requirement is treated as directory only. The second sentence of Rule 7.2 may assist the arbitrator here as it refers to documents *referred to* in Rule 7.3 being adduced as evidence at the hearing rather than any requirement that they have been identified to, or served on, the other party in accordance with Rule 7.3. Furthermore, to simply accept the documents late will not of itself be a ground for attacking the award – Rule 12.2.

Even if the arbitrator has power to allow the documents in, though they may be identified or served late, his problems may not be over. On the one hand a party must not be taken by surprise by the late introduction of documents, and on the other hand, the hearing must take place within 21 days of the preliminary meeting, so that cancelling and re-fixing the hearing will be contrary to the Rules if it takes the hearing outside the 21 day period. However, if the arbitrator chose to do this his award could probably not be challenged on this technical ground alone – Rule 12.2.

If the arbitrator felt particularly nervous about breaching Rule 7 in this way, he may consider switching to Rule 6 (full procedure with a hearing) pursuant to Rule 12.3 and then directing under Rule 6.2 that the Rule 6.3 statements should not be required, and then to fix a convenient hearing date. This, however, seems to be using a sledgehammer to crack a nut.

As is only to be expected where the Rules seek understandably to be brief and to the point, Rule 7.3, if analysed too deeply, raises a host of ambiguities. A few examples only will suffice:

● If one party only has a document which supports the other party's oral submission there appears to be no procedure within Rule 7.3 by which it is copied to the party seeking it, even where he clearly identifies it as being a necessary document. Perhaps a telephone call or a letter to the arbitrator, copied to the other party, identifying the document, with the request for a direction under Rule 7.4 or Rule 12.1.7 may be the answer if it is done quickly.

● The reference to *'document'* in the third line of Rule 7.3.1 presumably includes a copy document as well as an original. In other words, if a party already has an original or a copy in his possession he need not be served with a further copy.

• It is presumably the original documents, where relevant, rather than copies, which must be available at the hearing despite the wording of Rule 7.3.2.

• There is no procedure laid down as to how to find out if the other party already has a document in his possession, so obviating the need to supply a copy.

Provided there exists a spirit of co-operation between the parties, which is quite likely where they have jointly decided that the Rule 7 procedure is to apply, the application of sound common sense will avoid any problems being experienced as a result of these or any other ambiguities in the wording of Rule 7.

The hearing

By virtue of Rule 7.2 the hearing is to take place within 21 days of the date when the Rule 7 procedure is agreed, that is, at the preliminary meeting.

As mentioned above, in a good number of instances, where the parties and the arbitrator are prepared to do so, the hearing can take place immediately after the preliminary meeting itself. The arbitrator can, if appropriate, make an inspection pursuant to Rule 8 between the preliminary meeting and the hearing having already considered the documentation supplied, preferably in advance of the preliminary meeting. Alternatively, the arbitrator may make the inspection immediately after the oral hearing. In either case he can give his award immediately.

As Rule 7.3 requires any necessary documents to be served not later than seven days before the hearing and as that seven day period will not as a rule commence before the preliminary meeting at which the Rule 7 procedure is agreed, the parties can by agreement provisionally gear themselves up for a hearing immediately after the preliminary meeting, as can the arbitrator by providing any documentation required under Rule 7.3 in advance of the preliminary meeting, on the basis that once the Rule 7 procedure has been agreed, Rule 7.3 will have been complied with in relation to the provision of documentation. Indeed the Rules – see Rule 4.2.2 – facilitates such a procedure, as the claimant can serve the documents along with his case in writing under that Rule. Provided there are no other relevant documents in the respondent's possession on which he wishes to rely, this will suffice to enable the hearing to take place immediately after the preliminary meeting in compliance with Rule 7.

The procedure to be adopted at the hearing is entirely flexible, as indeed it should be – see Rule 7.4. The documents, if any, necessary to support the oral submissions, can, and generally will, constitute evidence. Generally, (see the last sentence to Rule 7.2) there will be no oral evidence as such. However, this can be permitted if the arbitrator so directs or allows it.

While it is obviously right that maximum flexibility is provided as to the procedures to be adopted at the hearing, nevertheless it will be for the arbitrator to control the hearing and to prevent it becoming a shambles. The rules of natural justice apply. Each side must be given a fair opportunity to put its case and to comment upon the other party's case. Though strict rules of evidence do not apply to arbitration, nevertheless in the nature of things, arbitrators should be careful to prevent hearsay evidence being given undue weight and to treat with some caution an oral submission which contains factual contentions unsupported by evidence. In such a case, if the contentions are contested then, if expedient, each side could be allowed to adduce oral evidence. However, if a serious conflict arises a change to Rule 6 (full procedure with a hearing) may be necessary.

Inspection

Because of the nature of the disputes for which the Rule 7 procedure may often be suitable (namely, quality matters) it will quite often be appropriate under this procedure for the arbitrator to exercise his powers of inspection pursuant to Rule 8 to inspect relevant work. Such inspection does not form part of the hearing itself.

It will very often be the case under Rule 7 that the parties impliedly, if not expressly, expect the arbitrator to use his own knowledge or special experience or expertise, and in this sense the inspection and the arbitrator's conclusions drawn therefrom will form part of the evidence and will not merely be limited to identifying the work or understanding the issues. If the arbitrator intends to treat his inspection in this way he ought to tell the parties that he is so doing and invite them to comment if they wish to. This question of the arbitrator using the inspection as direct evidence is discussed in more detail in considering Rule 8 earlier – see page 45.

There is no reason why the arbitrator should not in connection with the Rule 7 procedure act, at least in part, inquisitorially by asking questions of the parties in order to explore the dispute.

Costs

Rule 7.1.2, provides that each party is to bear its own costs unless for special reasons the arbitrator at his discretion otherwise directs.

Clearly this is designed to discourage the parties from engaging lawyers or other representatives (for example, claims consultants) by requiring even the successful party to bear his own costs. Whether this is an overreaction in the Rules can be debated. If the Rule 7 procedure applies then there can never be more than 21 days between the preliminary meeting and the hearing so that lawyers and other representatives, if they are to play a part, would need to adopt a somewhat different role to that which is traditional in any event. There are no pleadings; there will be little or no oral evidence. In these circumstances the costs are likely to relatively small. However, they may be sufficiently significant to cause a successful party, whether represented or not, to feel aggrieved at not being able to recover them.

The fear behind Rule 7.1.2 could be that the presence of a lawyer at the relatively informal hearing is likely to impede the process of dispute resolution between commercial men by a commercial man, namely the arbitrator, with the consequent risk that the arbitrator may be intimidated or, at any rate, inhibited, thus leading to a decision to switch from the Rule 7 procedure to Rule 6 (full procedure with a hearing). The risk may be heightened where a party has consulted a lawyer for the first time after having already agreed to the application of the Rule 7 procedure for the conduct of the arbitration. However, if a party does take legal advice for the first time after having agreed to the operation of the Rule 7 procedure and as a consequence changes his mind and engages a lawyer with a view to sabotaging the Rule 7 procedure, there is little that the arbitrator may be able to do to prevent it and the fact that the party concerned must bear his own legal costs is unlikely to be treated by him as crucial.

The arbitrator has a discretion to order one party to pay the other party's costs for 'special reasons'. There is no guidance in the Rules as to the circumstances in which the arbitrator might exercise this discretion. However, the discretion must be exercised judicially, which provides some control. Most instances amounting to special reasons will relate to the reasonableness or unreasonableness of the way in which the case is conducted. An example might be where a party pursues a thoroughly bad point, engaging legal or other representatives to do so, thus leading the successful party to engage his own representation. In such circumstances the successful party might be awarded his costs. Another example may be where one party is discovered to have deliberately sought to mislead the arbitrator.

The provisions of Rule 7.1.2 restricting the ordering of costs could lead to a party choosing not to agree to the application of the Rule 7 procedure even where it is ideal for the resolution of the particular dispute, e.g. where the other party has the benefit of an in-house lawyer who will get a salary in any event, that is, it will cost one party no more to use a lawyer than not to. Here the party without an in-house lawyer may feel that he is being treated unfairly in the Rule 7 procedure and will not opt for it on these grounds. If common sense prevails among the parties, however, this problem should not be a common one.

Costs in Rule 7.1.2 probably excludes the arbitrator's own fees and expenses. It would appear from Rule 9.3 that the arbitrator can order one party to be responsible for all of the arbitrator's fees and expenses even where the Rule 7 procedure applies.

The award

Rule 7.5 provides that at the end of the hearing the arbitrator shall either thereupon make his award or publish it within seven days. If the award is made orally at the end of the hearing the arbitrator must forthwith confirm his award in writing. The arbitrator may however publish his award later than the seven day period. If he chooses to do so he must, prior to the expiry of the seven days, immediately notify the parties in writing when his award will be published.

Clearly where the Rule 7 procedure applies the arbitrator should do everything within his power to publish his award promptly, lest the objective of speed in using the Rule 7 procedure be jeopardised.

If the award is given orally, that is, a parol award is made at the end of the hearing, it is valid even if it is never confirmed in writing.

Though unlikely to be made use of bearing in mind the nature of disputes which are amenable to the Rule 7 procedure, together with the provisions of the last paragraph of Rule 7.5 and the effect of Rule 12.2, the High Court has power under section 13(2) of the 1950 Act to enlarge the time within which the arbitrator can make his award.

Appendix 1

Arbitration Act 1950
(excluding schedules)

PART I

GENERAL PROVISIONS AS TO ARBITRATION

Effect of Arbitration Agreements, etc.

Authority of arbitrators and umpires to be irrevocable
   1.—The authority of an arbitrator or umpire appointed by or by virtue of an arbitration agreement shall, unless a contrary intention is expressed in the agreement, be irrevocable except by leave of the High Court or a judge thereof.

Death of party
   2.—(1) An arbitration agreement shall not be discharged by the death of any party thereto, either as respects the deceased or any other party, but shall in such an event be enforceable by or against the personal representative of the deceased.

   (2) The authority of an arbitrator shall not be revoked by the death of any party by whom he was appointed.

   (3) Nothing in this section shall be taken to affect the operation of any enactment or rule of law by virtue of which any right of action is extinguished by the death of a person.

Bankruptcy
   3.—(1) Where it is provided by a term in a contract to which a bankrupt is a party that any differences arising thereout or in connection therewith shall be referred to arbitration, the said term shall, if the trustee in bankruptcy adopts the contract, be enforceable by or against him so far as relates to any such differences.

   (2) Where a person who has been adjudged bankrupt had, before the commencement of the bankruptcy, become a party to an arbitration agreement, and any matter to which the agreement applies requires to be determined in connection with or for the purposes of the bankruptcy proceedings, then, if the case is one to which subsection (1) of this section does not apply, any other party to the agreement or, with the

consent of the committee of inspection, the trustee in bankruptcy, may apply to the court having jurisdiction in the bankruptcy proceedings for an order directing that the matter in question shall be referred to arbitration in accordance with the agreement, and that court may, if it is of opinion that, having regard to all the circumstances of the case, the matter ought to be determined by arbitration, make an order accordingly.

Staying court proceedings where there is submission to arbitration
   4.—(1) If any party to an arbitration agreement, or any person claiming through or under him, commences any legal proceedings in any court against any other party to the agreement, or any person claiming through or under him, in respect of any matter agreed to be referred, any party to those legal proceedings may at any time after appearance, and before delivering any pleadings or taking any other steps in the proceedings, apply to that court to stay the proceedings, and that court or a judge thereof, if satisfied that there is no sufficient reason why the matter should not be referred in accordance with the agreement, and that the applicant was, at the time when the proceedings were commenced, and still remains, ready and willing to do all things necessary to the proper conduct of the arbitration, may make an order staying the proceedings.
   (2)[*Repealed by Arbitration Act 1975, s.8(2)(a)*]

Reference of interpleader issues to arbitration
   5. Where relief by way of interpleader is granted and it appears to the High Court that the claims in question are matters to which an arbitration agreement, to which the claimants are parties, applies, the High Court may direct the issue between the claimants to be determined in accordance with the agreement.

Arbitrators and Umpires

When reference is to a single arbitrator
   6. Unless a contrary intention is expressed therein, every arbitration agreement shall, if no other mode of reference is provided, be deemed to include a provision that the reference shall be to a single arbitrator.

Power of parties in certain cases to supply vacancy
   7. Where an arbitration agreement provides that the reference shall be two arbitrators, one to be appointed by each party, then, unless a contrary intention is expressed therein—

   (*a*) if either of the appointed arbitrators refuses to act, or is incapable of acting, or dies, the party who appointed him may appoint a new arbitrator in his place;

   (*b*) if, on such a reference, one party fails to appoint an arbitrator, either originally, or by way of substitution as aforesaid, for seven clear days after the other party, having appointed his arbitrator, has served the party making default with notice to make the appointment, the party who has appointed an arbitrator may appoint that arbitrator to act as sole arbitrator in the reference and his award shall be binding on both parties as if he had been appointed by consent:

Provided that the High Court or a judge thereof may set aside any appointment made in pursuance of this section.

Umpires

8.—(1) Unless a contrary intention is expressed therein, every arbitration agreement shall, where the reference is to two, arbitrators, be deemed to include a provision that the two arbitrators may appoint an umpire at any time after they are themselves appointed and shall do so forthwith if they cannot agree.

(2) Unless a contrary intention is expressed therein, every arbitration agreement shall, where such a provision is applicable to the reference, be deemed to include a provision that if the arbitrators have delivered to any party to the arbitration agreement, or to the umpire, a notice in writing stating that they cannot agree, the umpire may forthwith enter on the reference in lieu of the arbitrators.

(3) At any time after the appointment of an umpire, however appointed, the High Court may, on the application of any party to the reference and notwithstanding anything to the contrary in the arbitration agreement, order that the umpire shall enter upon the reference in lieu of the arbitrators and as if he were a sole arbitrator.

[Majority Award of Three Arbitrators

9. Unless the contrary intention is expressed in the arbitration agreement, in any case where there is a reference to three arbitrators, the award of any two of the arbitrators shall be binding.]

[Substituted by Arbitration Act 1979, s.6(2).]

Power of court in certain cases to appoint an arbitrator or umpire

10. In any of the following cases—

(a) where an arbitration agreement provides that the reference shall be to a single arbitrator, and all the parties do not, after differences have arisen, concur in the appointment of an arbitrator;

(b) if an appointed arbitrator refuses to act, or is incapable of acting or dies, and the arbitration agreement does not show that it was intended that the vacancy should not be supplied and the parties do not supply the vacancy;

(c) where the parties or two arbitrators are required or are at liberty to appoint an umpire or third arbitrator and do not appoint him;

(*d*) where an appointed umpire or third arbitrator refuses to act, or is incapable of acting, or dies, and the arbitration agreement does not show that it was intended that the vacancy should not be supplied, and the parties or arbitrators do not supply the vacancy;

any party may serve the other parties or the arbitrators, as the case may be, with a written notice to appoint or, as the case may be, concur in appointing, an arbitrator, umpire or third arbitrator, and if the appointment is not made within seven clear days after the service of the notice, the High Court or a judge thereof may, on application by the party who gave the notice, appoint an arbitrator, umpire or third arbitrator who shall have the like powers to act in the reference and make an award as if he had been appointed by consent of all parties.

[(2) In any case where—

(*a*) an arbitration agreement provides for the appointment of an arbitrator or umpire by a person who is neither one of the parties nor an existing arbitrator (whether the provision applies directly or in default of agreement by the parties or otherwise), and

(*b*) that person refuses to make the appointment or does not make it within the time specified in the agreement or, if no time is so specified, within a reasonable time.

any party to the agreement may serve the person in question with a written notice to appoint an arbitrator or umpire and, if the appointment is not made within seven clear days after the service of the notice, the High Court or a judge thereof may, on the application of the party who gave the notice, appoint an arbitrator or umpire who shall have the like powers to act in the reference and make an award as if he had been appointed in accordance with the terms of the agreement].

(3) In any case where—

(a) an arbitration agreement provides that the reference shall be to three arbitrators, one to be appointed by each party and the third to be appointed by the two appointed by the parties or in some other manner specified in the agreement; and

(b) one of the parties 'the party in default' refuses to appoint an arbitrator or does not do so within the time specified in the agreement or, if no time is specified, within a reasonable time,

the other party to the agreement, having appointed his arbitrator, may serve the party in default with a written notice to appoint an arbitrator and, if the appointment is not made within seven clear days after the service of the notice, the High Court or a judge thereof may, on the application of the party who gave the notice, appoint an arbitrator on behalf of the party in default who shall have the like powers to act in the reference and make an award (and, if the case so requires, the like duty in relation to the appointment of a third arbitrator) as if he had been appointed in accordance with the terms of the agreement.

(4) Except in a case where the arbitration agreement shows that it was intended that the vacancy should not be supplied, paragraph (b) of each of subsections (2) and (3) shall be construed as extending to any such refusal or failure by a person as is there mentioned arising in connection with the replacement of an arbitrator who was appointed by that person (or, in default of being so appointed, was appointed under that subsection) but who refuses to act, or is incapable of acting or has died.

Reference to official referee

11. Where an arbitration agreement provides that the reference shall be to an official referee, any official referee to whom application is made shall, subject to any order of the High Court or a judge thereof as to transfer or otherwise, hear and determine the matters agreed to be referred.

Conduct of Proceedings, Witnesses, etc.

Conduct of proceedings, witnesses, etc.

12.—(1) Unless a contrary intention is expressed therein, every arbitration agreement shall, where such a provision is applicable to the reference, be deemed to contain a provision that the parties to the reference, and all persons claiming through them respectively, shall, subject to any legal objection, submit to be examined by the arbitrator or umpire, on oath or affirmation, in relation to the matters in dispute, and shall, subject as aforesaid, produce before the arbitrator or umpire all documents within their possession or power respectively which may be required or called for, and do all other things which during the proceedings on the reference the arbitrator or umpire may require.

(2) Unless a contrary intention is expressed therein, every arbitration agreement shall, where such a provision is applicable to the reference, be deemed to contain a provision that the witnesses on the reference shall, if the arbitrator or umpire thinks fit, be examined on oath or affirmation.

(3) An arbitrator or umpire shall, unless a contrary intention is expressed in the arbitration agreement, have power to administer oaths to, or take the affirmations of, the parties to and witnesses on a reference under the agreement.

(4) Any party to a reference under an arbitration agreement may sue out a writ of subpoena ad testificandum or a writ of subpoena duces tecum, but no person shall be compelled under any such writ to produce any document which he could not be compelled to produce on the trial of an action, and the High Court or a judge thereof may order that a writ of subpoena ad testificandum or of subpoena duces tecum shall issue to compel the attendance before an arbitrator or umpire of a witness wherever he may be within the United Kingdom.

(5) The High Court or a judge thereof may also order that a writ of habeas corpus ad testificandum shall issue to bring up a prisoner for examination before an arbitrator or umpire.

(6) The High Court shall have, for the purpose of and in relation to a reference, the same power of making orders in respect of—

(*a*) security for costs;

(*b*) discovery of documents and interrogatories;

(*c*) the giving of evidence by affidavit;

(*d*) examination on oath of any witness before an officer of the High Court or any other person, and the issue of a commission or request for the examination of a witness out of the jurisdiction;

(*e*) the preservation, interim custody or sale of any goods which are the subject matter of the reference;

(*f*) securing the amount in dispute in the reference;

(*g*) the detention, preservation or inspection of any property or thing which is the subject of the reference or as to which any question may arise therein, and authorising for any of the purposes aforesaid any persons to enter upon or into any land or building in the possession of any party to the reference, or authorising any samples to be taken or any observation to be made or experiment to be tried which may be necessary or expedient for the purpose of obtaining full information or evidence; and

(*h*) interim injunctions or the appointment of a receiver;

as it has for the purpose of and in relation to an action or matter in the High Court:

Provided that nothing in this subsection shall be taken to prejudice any power which may be vested in an arbitrator or umpire of making orders with respect to any of the matters aforesaid.

Provisions as to Awards

Time for making award

13.—(1) Subject to the provisions of subsection (2) of section twenty-two of this Act, and anything to the contrary in the arbitration agreement, an arbitrator or umpire shall have power to make an award at any time.

(2) The time, if any, limited for making an award, whether under this Act or otherwise, may from time to time be enlarged by order of the High Court or a judge thereof, whether that time has expired or not.

(3) The High Court may, on the application of any party to a reference, remove an arbitrator or umpire who fails to use all reasonable dispatch in entering on and proceeding with the reference and making an award, and an arbitrator or umpire who is removed by the High Court under this subsection shall not be entitled to receive any remuneration in respect of his services.

For the purposes of this subsection, the expression 'proceeding with a reference' includes, in a case where two arbitrators are unable to agree, giving notice of the fact to the parties and to the umpire.

Interim awards

14. Unless a contrary intention is expressed therein, every arbitration agreement shall, where such a provision is applicable to the reference, be deemed to contain a provision that the arbitrator or umpire may, if he thinks fit, make an interim award, and any reference in this Part of the Act to an award includes a reference to an interim award.

Specific performance

15. Unless a contrary intention is expressed therein, every arbitration agreement shall, where such a provision is applicable to the reference, be deemed to contain a provision that the arbitrator or umpire shall have the same power as the High Court to order specific performance of any contract other than a contract relating to land or any interest in land.

Awards to be final

16. Unless a contrary intention is expressed therein, every arbitration agreement shall, where such a provision is applicable to the reference, be deemed to contain a provision that the award to be made by the arbitrator or umpire shall be final and binding on the parties and the persons claiming under them respectively.

Power to correct slips

17. Unless a contrary intention is expressed in the arbitration agreement, the arbitrator or umpire shall have power to correct in an award any clerical mistake or error arising from any accidental slip or omission.

Costs, Fees and Interest

Costs

18.—(1) Unless a contrary intention is expressed therein, every arbitration agreement shall be deemed to include a provision that the costs of the reference and award shall be in the discretion of the arbitrator or umpire, who may direct to and by whom and in what manner those costs or any part thereof shall be paid, and may tax or settle the amount of costs to be so paid or any part thereof, and may award costs to be paid as between solicitor and client.

(2) Any costs directed by an award to be paid shall, unless the award otherwise directs, be taxable in the High Court.

(3) Any provision in an arbitration agreement to the effect that the parties or any party thereto shall in any event pay their or his own costs of the reference or award or any part thereof shall be void, and this Part of this Act, shall in the case of an arbitration agreement containing any

such provision, have effect as if that provision were not contained therein:

Provided that nothing in this subsection shall invalidate such a provision when it is a part of an agreement to submit to arbitration a dispute which has arisen before the making of that agreement.

(4) If no provision is made by an award with respect to the costs of the reference, any party to the reference may, within fourteen days of the publication of the award or such further time as the High Court or a judge thereof may direct, apply to the arbitrator for an order directing by and to whom those costs shall be paid, and thereupon the arbitrator shall, after hearing any party who may desire to be heard, amend his award by adding thereto such directions as he may think proper with respect to the payment of the costs of the reference.

(5) Section sixty-nine of the Solicitors Act 1932 (which empowers a court before which any proceeding is being heard or is pending to charge property recovered or preserved in the proceeding with the payment of solicitors' costs) shall apply as if an arbitration were a proceeding in the High Court and the High Court may make declarations and orders accordingly.

Taxation of arbitrator's or umpire's fees

19.—(1) If in any case an arbitrator or umpire refuses to deliver his award except on payment of the fees demanded by him, the High Court may, on an application for the purpose, order that the arbitrator or umpire shall deliver the award to the applicant on payment into court by the applicant of the fees demanded, and further that the fees demanded shall be taxed by the taxing officer and that out of the money paid into court there shall be paid out to the arbitrator or umpire by way of fees such sums as may be found reasonable on taxation and that the balance of the money, if any, shall be paid out to the applicant.

(2) An application for the purpose of this section may be made by any party to the reference unless the fees demanded have been fixed by a written agreement between him and the arbitrator or umpire.

(3) A taxation of fees under this section may be reviewed in the same manner as a taxation of costs.

(4) The arbitrator or umpire shall be entitled to appear and be heard on any taxation or review of taxation under this section.

Power of arbitrator to award interest

19A.—(1) Unless a contrary intention is expressed therein, every arbitration agreement shall, where such a provision is applicable to the reference, be deemed to contain a provision that the arbitrator or umpire may, if he thinks fit, award simple interest at such rate as he thinks fit—

(*a*) on any sum which is the subject of the reference but which is paid before the award, for such period ending not later than the date of the payment as he thinks fit; and (*b*) on any sum which he awards, for such period ending not later than the date of the award as he thinks fit.

(2) The power to award interest conferred on an arbitrator or umpire by subsection (1) above is without prejudice to any other power of an arbitrator or umpire to award interest.

Interest on awards
20. A sum directed to be paid by an award shall, unless the award otherwise directs, carry interest as from the date of the award and at the same rate as a judgment debt.

Special Cases, Remission and Setting aside of Awards, etc.

Statement of case
21.—Repealed by Arbitration Act 1979

Power to remit award
22.—(1) In all cases of reference to arbitration the High Court or a judge thereof may from time to time remit the matters referred, or any of them, to the reconsideration of the arbitrator or umpire.

(2) Where an award is remitted, the arbitrator or umpire shall, unless the order otherwise directs, make his award within three months after the date of the order.

Removal of arbitrator and setting aside of award
23.—(1) Where an arbitrator or umpire has misconducted himself or the proceedings, the High Court may remove him.

(2) Where an arbitrator or umpire has misconducted himself or the proceedings, or an arbitration or award has been properly procured the High Court may set the award aside.

(3) Where an application is made to set aside an award, the High Court may order that any money made payable by the award shall be brought into court or otherwise secured pending the determination of the application.

Power of court to give relief where arbitrator is not impartial or the dispute involves question of fraud
24.—(1) Where an agreement between any parties provides that disputes which may arise in the future between them shall be referred to an arbitrator named or designated in the agreement, and after a dispute has arisen any party applies, on the ground that the arbitrator so named or designated is not or may not be impartial, for leave to revoke the authority of the arbitrator or for an injunction to restrain any other party or the arbitrator from proceedings with the arbitration, it shall not be a ground for refusing the application that the said party at the time when he made the agreement knew, or ought to have known, that the

arbitrator, by reason of his relation towards any other party to the agreement or of his connection with the subject referred, might not be capable of impartiality.

(2) Where an agreement between any parties provides that disputes which may arise in the future between them shall be referred to arbitration, and a dispute which so arises involves the question whether any such party has been guilty of fraud, the High Court shall, so far as may be necessary to enable that question to be determined by the High Court, have power to order that the agreement shall cease to have effect and power to give leave to revoke the authority of any arbitrator or umpire appointed by or by virtue of the agreement.

(3) In any case where by virtue of this section the High Court has power to order that an arbitration agreement shall ceased to have effect or to give leave to revoke the authority of an arbitrator or umpire the High Court may refuse to stay any action brought in breach of the agreement.

Power of court where arbitrator is removed or authority of arbitrator is revoked

25.—(1) Where an arbitrator (not being a sole arbitrator), or two or more arbitrators (not being all the arbitrators) or an umpire who has not entered on the reference is or are removed by the High Court or the Court of Appeal, the High Court or the Court of Appeal as the case may be, may, on the application of any party to the arbitration agreement, appoint a person or persons to act as arbitrator or arbitrators or umpire in place of the person or persons so removed.

(2) Where the authority of an arbitrator or arbitrators or umpire is revoked by leave of the High Court or the Court of Appeal, or a sole arbitrator or all the arbitrators or an umpire who has entered on the reference is or are removed by the High Court or the Court of Appeal, the High Court or the Court of Appeal as the case may be, may, on the application of any party to the arbitration agreement, either—

(a) appoint a person to act as sole arbitrator in place of the person or persons removed; or

(b) order that the arbitration agreement shall cease to have effect with respect to the dispute referred.

(3) A person appointed under this section by the High Court or the Court of Appeal as an arbitrator or umpire shall have the like power to act in the reference and to make an award as if he had been appointed in accordance with the terms of the arbitration agreement.

(4) Where it is provided (whether by means of a provision in the arbitration agreement or otherwise) that an award under an arbitration agreement shall be a condition precedent to the bringing of an action with respect to any matter to which the agreement applies, the High Court or the Court of Appeal, if it orders (whether under this section or under any other enactment) that the agreement shall cease to have effect

as regards any particular dispute, may further order that the provision making an award a condition precedent to the bringing of an action shall also cease to have effect as regards that dispute.

Enforcement of Award

Enforcement of award
   26.—(1) An award on an arbitration agreement may, by leave of the High Court or a judge thereof, be enforced in the same manner as a judgment or order to the same effect, and where leave is so given, judgment may be entered in terms of the award.
   [(2) If—

(a) the amount sought to be recovered does not exceed the current limit on jurisdiction in section 40 of the County Courts Act 1959, and
(b) a county court so orders,

it shall be recoverable (by execution issued from the county court or otherwise) as if payable under an order of that court and shall not be enforceable under subsection (1) above.
   (3) An application to the High Court under this section shall preclude an application to a county court and an application to a county court under this section shall preclude an application to the High Court.]

Miscellaneous

Power of court to extend time for commencing arbitration proceedings
   27. Where the terms of an agreement to refer future disputes to arbitration provide that any claims to which the agreement applies shall be barred unless notice to appoint an arbitrator is given or an arbitrator is appointed or some other step to commence arbitration proceedings is taken within a time fixed by the agreement, and a dispute arises to which the agreement applies, the High Court, if it is of opinion that in the circumstances of the case undue hardship would otherwise be caused, and notwithstanding that the time so fixed has expired, may, on such terms, if any, as the justice of the case may require, but without prejudice to the provisions of any enactment limiting the time for the commencement of arbitration proceedings, extend the time for such period as it thinks proper.

Terms as to costs, etc.
   28. Any order made under this Part of this Act may be made on such terms as to costs or otherwise as the authority making the order thinks just.

Extension of section 496 of the Merchant Shipping Act 1894
   29.—(1) In subsection (3) of section four hundred and ninety-six of the

Merchant Shipping Act 1894 (which requires a sum deposited with a wharfinger by an owner of goods to be repaid unless legal proceedings are instituted by the shipowner), the expression 'legal proceedings' shall be deemed to include arbitration.

(2) For the purposes of the said section four hundred and ninety-six, as amended by this section, an arbitration shall be deemed to be commenced when one party to the arbitration agreement serves on the other party or parties a notice requiring him or them to appoint or concur in appointing an arbitrator, or, where the arbitration agreement provides that the reference shall be to a person named or designated in the agreement, requiring him or them to submit the dispute to the person so named or designated.

(3) Any such notice as is mentioned in subsection (2) of this section may be served either—

(a) by delivering it to the person on whom it is to be served; or
(b) by leaving it at the usual or last known place of abode in England of that person; or
(c) by sending it by post in a registered letter addressed to that person at his usual or last known place of abode in England;

as well as in any other manner provided in the arbitration agreement; and where a notice is sent by post in manner prescribed by paragraph (c) of this subsection, service thereof shall, unless the contrary is proved, be deemed to have been effected at the time at which the letter would have been delivered in the ordinary course of post.

Crown to be bound
   30. This part of this Act [. . .] shall apply to any arbitration to which his Majesty, either in right of the Crown or of the Duchy of Lancaster or otherwise, or the Duke of Cornwall, is a party.

Application of Part I to statutory arbitrations
   31.—(1) Subject to the provisions of section thirty-three of this Act, this Part of this Act, expect the provisions thereof specified in subsection (2) of this section, shall apply to every arbitration under any other Act (whether passed before or after the commencement of this Act) as if the arbitration were pursuant to an arbitration agreement and as if that other Act were an arbitration agreement, except in so far as this Act is inconsistent with that other Act or with any rules or procedure authorised or recognised thereby.

(2) The provisions referred to in subsection (1) of this section are subsection (1) of section two, section three (*words deleted by Arbitration Act 1975, s.8(2)(d)*), section five, subsection (3) of section eighteen and sections twenty-four, twenty-five, twenty-seven and twenty-nine.

Meaning of 'arbitration agreement'
   32. In this Part of this Act, unless the context otherwise requires, the

expression 'arbitration agreement' means a written agreement to submit present or future differences to arbitration, whether an arbitrator is named therein or not.

Operation of Part I

33. This Part of this Act shall not affect any arbitration commenced (within the meaning of subsection (2) of section twenty-nine of this Act) before the commencement of this Act, but shall apply to an arbitration so commenced after the commencement of this Act under an agreement made before the commencement of this Act.

Extent of Part I

34. [. . .] Save as aforesaid, none of the provisions of this Part of this Act shall extend to Scotland or Northern Ireland.

Part II

Enforcement of Certain Foreign Awards

Awards to which Part II applies

35.—(1) This Part of this Act applies to any award made after the twenty-eighth day of July, nineteen hundred and twenty-four—

(a) in pursuance of an agreement for arbitration to which the protocol set out in the First Schedule to this Act applies; and

(b) between persons of whom one is subject to the jurisdiction of some one of such Powers as His Majesty, being satisfied that reciprocal provisions have been made, may by Order in Council declare to be parties to the convention set out in the Second Schedule to this Act, and of whom the other is subject to the jurisdiction of some other of the Powers aforesaid; and

(c) in one of such territories as His Majesty, being satisfied that reciprocal provisions have been made, may by Order in Council declare to be territories to which the said convention applies;

and an award to which this Part of this Act applies is in this Part of this Act referred to as 'a foreign award.'

(2) His Majesty may be a subsequent Order in Council vary or revoke any Order previously made under this section.

(3) Any Order in Council under section one of the Arbitration (Foreign Awards) Act 1930, which is in force at the commencement of this Act shall have effect as if it had been made under this section.

Effect of foreign awards

36.—(1) A foreign award shall, subject to the provisions of this Part of this Act, be enforceable in England either by action or in the same manner as the award of an arbitrator is enforceable by virtue of section twenty-six of this Act.

(2) Any foreign award which would be enforceable under this Part of this Act shall be treated as binding for all purposes on the persons as between whom it was made, and may accordingly be relied on by any of those persons by way of defence, set off or otherwise in any legal proceedings in England, and any references in this Part of this Act to enforcing a foreign award shall be construed as including references to relying on an award.

Conditions for enforcement of foreign awards

37.—(1) In order that a foreign award may be enforceable under this part of this Act it must have—

 (a) been made in pursuance of an agreement for arbitration which was valid under the law by which it was governed;
 (b) been made by the tribunal provided for in the agreement or constituted in manner agreed upon by the parties;
 (c) been made in conformity with the law governing the arbitration procedure;
 (d) become final in the country in which it was made;
 (e) been in respect of a matter which may lawfully be referred to arbitration under the law of England;

and the enforcement thereof must not be contrary to the public policy or the law of England.

(2) Subject to the provisions of this subsection, a foreign award shall not be enforceable under this Part of this Act if the court dealing with the case is satisfied that—

 (a) the award has been annulled in the country in which it was made; or
 (b) the party against whom it is sought to enforce the award was not given notice of the arbitration proceedings in sufficient time to enable him to present his case, or was under some legal incapacity and was not properly represented; or
 (c) the award does not deal with all the questions referred or contains decisions on matters beyond the scope of the agreement for arbitration:

Provided that, if the award does not deal with all the questions referred, the court may, if it thinks fit, either postpone the enforcement of the award or order its enforcement subject to the giving of such security by the person seeking to enforce it as the court may think fit.

(3) If a party seeking to resist the enforcement of a foreign award proves that there is any ground other than the non-existence of the conditions specified in paragraphs (a), (b), and (c) of subsection (1) of this section, or the existence of the conditions specified in paragraphs (b) and (c) of subsection (2) of this section, entitling him to contest the validity of the award, the court may, if it thinks fit, either refuse to enforce the award or adjourn the hearing until after the expiration of such period as appears to the court to be reasonably sufficient to enable

that party to take the necessary steps to have the award annulled by the competent tribunal.

Evidence
38.—(1) The party seeking to enforce a foreign award must produce—

(a) the original award or a copy thereof duly authenticated in manner required by the law of the country in which it was made; and
(b) evidence proving that the award has become final; and
(c) such evidence as may be necessary to prove that the award is a foreign award and that the conditions mentioned in paragraphs (a), (b), and (c) of subsection (1) of the last foregoing section are satisfied.

(2) In any case where any document required to be produced under subsection (1) of this section is in a foreign language, it shall be the duty of the party seeking to enforce the award to produce a translation certified as correct by a diplomatic or consular agent of the country to which that party belongs, or certified as correct in such other manner as may be sufficient according to the law of England.

(3) Subject to the provisions of this section, rules of court may be made under section [84 of the Supreme Court Act 1981] with respect to the evidence which must be furnished by a party seeking to enforce an award under this Part of this Act.

Meaning of 'final award'
39. For the purposes of this Part of this Act, an award shall not be deemed final if any proceedings for the purpose of contesting the validity of the award are pending in the country in which it was made.

Saving for rights, etc.
40. Nothing in this Part of this Act shall—

(a) prejudice any rights which any person would have had of enforcing in England any award or of availing himself in England of any award if neither this Part of this Act nor Part I of the Arbitration (Foreign Awards) Act 1930 had been enacted; or
(b) apply to any award made on an arbitration agreement governed by the law of England.

Application of Part II to Scotland
41.—(1) The following provisions of this section shall have the effect for the purpose of the application of this Part of this Act to Scotland.

(2) For the references to England there shall be substituted references to Scotland.

(3) For subsection (1) of section thirty-six there shall be substituted the following subsection:

'(1) A foreign award shall, subject to the provisions of this Part of this Act, be enforceable by action, or, if the agreement for arbitration contains consent to the registration of the award in the Books of Council and Session for the execution and the award is so registered, it shall, subject as aforesaid, be enforceable by summary diligence.'

(4) For subsections (3) of section thirty-eight there shall be substituted the following subsection:

'(3) The Court of Session shall, subject to the provisions of this section, have power to make provision by Act of Sederunt with respect to the evidence which must be furnished by a party seeking to enforce in Scotland an award under this Part of this Act.'

Application of Part II to Northern Ireland
42.—(1) The following provisions of this section shall have effect for the purpose of the application of this Part of this Act to Northern Ireland.

(2) For the references to England there shall be substituted references to Northern Ireland.

(3) For subsection (1) of section thirty-six there shall be substituted the following subsection:—

(1) A foreign award shall, subject to the provisions of this Part of this Act, be enforceable either by action or in the same manner as the award of an arbitrator under the provisions of the Common Law Procedure Amendment Act (Ireland) 1856 was enforceable at the date of the passing of the Arbitration (Foreign Awards) Act 1930.'

(4) [*Repealed by Judicature (Northern Ireland) Act 1978, Sched. 7.*]

Saving for pending proceedings
43. [*Repealed by the Statute Law (Repeals) Act 1978, Sched. 1.*]

PART III

GENERAL

Short title, commencement and repeal
44.—(1) This Act may be cited as the Arbitration Act 1950.

(2) This Act shall come into operation on the first day of September, nineteen hundred and fifty.

(3) The Arbitration Act 1889, the Arbitration Clauses (Protocol) Act 1924 and the Arbitration Act 1934 are hereby repealed except in relation to arbitrations commenced (within the meaning of subsection (2) of section twenty-nine of this Act) before the commencement of this Act, and the Arbitration (Foreign Awards) Act 1930 is hereby repealed; and any reference in any Act or other document to any enactment hereby repealed shall be construed as including a reference to the corresponding provision of this Act.

Appendix 2

Arbitration Act 1979

Judicial review of arbitration awards

1.—(1) In the Arbitration Act 1950 (in this Act referred to as 'the principal Act') section 21 (statement of case for a decision of the High Court) shall cease to have effect and, without prejudice to the right of appeal conferred by subsection (2) below, the High Court shall not have jurisdiction to set aside or remit an award on an arbitration agreement on the ground of errors of fact or law on the face of the award.

(2) Subject to subsection (3) below, an appeal shall lie to the High Court on any question of law arising out of an award made on an arbitration agreement; and on the determination of such an appeal the High Court may by order—

(a) confirm, vary or set aside the award; or

(b) remit the award to the reconsideration of the arbitrator or umpire together with the court's opinion on the question of law which was the subject of the appeal;

and where the award is remitted under paragraph (b) above the arbitrator or umpire shall, unless the order otherwise directs, make his award within three months after the date of the order.

(3) An appeal under this section may be brought by any of the parties to the reference—

(a) with the consent of all the other parties to the reference; or

(b) subject to section 3 below, with the leave of the court.

(4) The High Court shall not grant leave under subsection (3)(b) above unless it considers that, having regard to all the circumstances, the determination of the question of law concerned could substantially affect the rights of one or more of the parties to the arbitration agreement; and the court may make any leave which it gives conditional upon the applicant complying with such conditions as it considers appropriate.

(5) Subject to subsection (6) below, if an award is made and, on an application made by any of the parties to the reference,—

(a) with the consent of all the other parties to the reference, or

(b) subject to section 3 below, with the leave of the court, it appears to the High Court that the award does not or does not sufficiently set out the reasons for the award, the court may order the arbitrator or umpire concerned to state the reasons for his award in sufficient detail to enable the court, should an appeal be brought under this section, to consider any question of law arising out of the award.

(6) In any case where an award is made without any reason being given, the High Court shall not make an order under subsection (5) above unless it is satisfied—

(*a*) that before the award was made one of the parties to the reference gave notice to the arbitrator or umpire concerned that a reasoned award would be required; or

(*b*) that there is some special reason why such a notice was not given.

[(6A) Unless the High Court gives leave, no appeal shall lie to the Court of Appeal from a decision of the High Court—

(*a*) to grant or refuse leave under subsection (3)(*b*) or (5)(*b*) above; or

(*b*) to make or not to make an order under subsection (5) above.

(7) No appeal shall lie to the Court of Appeal from a decision of the High Court of an appeal under this section unless—

(*a*) the High Court or the Court of Appeal gives leave; and

(*b*) it is certified by the High Court that the question of law to which its decision relates either is one of general public importance or is one which for some other special reason should be considered by the Court of Appeal.

(8) Where the award of an arbiter or umpire is varied on appeal, the award as varied shall have effect (except for the purposes of this section) as if it were the award of the arbitrator or umpire.

Subs. (6A) added by the Supreme Court Act 1981, s.148(1). This amendment does not apply to decisions of the High Court pronounced before January 1, 1982.

Determination of preliminary point of law by court

2.—(1) Subject to subsection (2) and section (3) below, on an application to the High Court made by any of the parties to a reference—

(*a*) with the consent of an arbitrator who has entered on the reference or, if an umpire has entered on the reference, with his consent, or

(*b*) with the consent of all the other parties.

the High Court shall have jurisdiction to determine any question of law arising in the course of the reference.

(2) The High Court shall not entertain an application under subsection (1)(*a*) above with respect to any question of law unless it is satisfied that—

(*a*) the determination of the application might produce substantial savings in costs to the parties; and (*b*) the question of law is one in respect of which leave to appeal would be likely to be given under section 1(3)(*b*) above.

[(2A) Unless the High Court gives leave, no appeal shall lie to the Court of Appeal from a decision of the High Court to entertain or not to entertain an application under subsection (1)(*a*) above.]

(3) A decision of the High Court under [subsection (1) above] shall be deemed to be a judgment of the court within the meaning of section [16 of the Supreme Court Act 1981] (appeals to the Court of Appeal), but no appeal shall lie from such a decision unless—

(*a*) the High Court or the Court of Appeal gives leave; and
(*b*) it is certified by the High Court that the question of law to which its decision relates either is one of general public importance or is one which for some other special reason should be considered by the Court of Appeal.

Subs. (2A) added by the Supreme Court Act 1981, s.148(1).
Subs. (3) amended by *ibid.*, s.152(1) and Sched. 5.

Exclusion agreements affecting rights under sections (1) and (2)

3.—(1) Subject to the following provisions of this section and section 4 below—

(*a*) the High Court shall not, under section 1(3)(*b*) above, grant leave to appeal with respect to a question of law arising out of an award, and
(*b* the High Court shall not, under section 1(5)(*b*) above, grant leave to make an application with respect to an award, and
(*c*) no application may be made under section 2(1)(*a*) above with respect to a question of law,

if the parties to the reference in question have entered into an agreement in writing (in this section referred to as an 'exclusion agreement') which excludes the right of appeal under section 1 above in relation to that award or, in a case falling within paragraph (*c*) above, in relation to an award to which the determination of the question of law is material.

(2) An exclusion agreement may be expressed so as to relate to a particular award, to awards under a particular reference or to any other description of awards, whether arising out of the same reference or not; and an agreement may be an exclusion agreement for the purposes of this section whether it is entered into before or after the passing of this Act and whether or not it forms part of an arbitration agreement.

(3) In any case where—

(*a*) an arbitration agreement, other than a domestic arbitration agreement, provides for disputes between the parties to be referred to arbitration, and
(*b*) a dispute to which the agreement relates involves the question whether a party has been guilty of fraud, and

(*c*) the parties have entered into an exclusion agreement which is applicable to any award made on the reference of that dispute.

then, except in so far as the exclusion agreement otherwise provides, the High Court shall not exercise its powers under section 24(2) of the principal Act (to take steps necessary to enable the question to be determined by the High Court) in relation to that dispute.

(4) Except as provided by subsection (1) above, sections 1 and 2 above shall have effect notwithstanding anything in any agreement purporting—

(*a*) to prohibit or restrict access to the High Court; or
(*b*) to restrict the jurisdiction of that court; or
(*c*) to prohibit or restrict the making of a reasoned award.

(5) An exclusion agreement shall be of no effect in relation to an award made on, or a question of law arising in the course of a reference under, a statutory arbitration, that is to say, such an arbitration as is referred to in subsection (1) of section 31 of the principal Act.

(6) An exclusion agreement shall be of no effect in relation to an award made on, or a question of law arising in the course of a reference under, an arbitration agreement which is a domestic arbitration agreement unless the exclusion agreement is entered into after the commencement of the arbitration in which the award is made or, as the case may be, in which the question of law arises.

(7) In this section 'domestic arbitration agreement' means an arbitration agreement which does not provide, expressly or by implication, for arbitration in a State other than the United Kingdom and to which neither—

(*a*) an individual who is a national of, or habitually resident in, any State other than the United Kingdom, nor
(*b*) a body corporate which is incorporated in, or whose central management and control is exercised in, any State other than the United Kingdom,

is a party at the time the arbitration agreement is entered into.

Exclusion agreements not to apply in certain cases
4.—(1) Subject to subsection (3) below, if an arbitration award or a question of law arising in the course of a reference relates, in whole or in part to—

(*a*) a question or claim falling within the Admiralty jurisdiction of the High Court, or
(*b*) a dispute arising out of a contract of insurance, or
(*c*) a dispute arising out of a commodity contract,

an exclusion agreement shall have no effect in relation to the award or question unless either—

(i) the exclusion agreement is entered into after the commencement of the arbitration in which the award is made or, as the case may be, in which the question of law arises, or

(ii) the award or question relates to a contract which is expressed to be governed by a law other than the law of England and Wales.

(2) In subsection (1)(*c*) above 'commodity contract' means a contract—

(*a*) for the sale of goods regularly dealt with on a commodity market or exchange in England or Wales which is specified for the purposes of this section by an order made by the Secretary of State; and

(*b*) of a description so specified.

(3) The Secretary of State may by order provide that subsection (1) above—

(*a*) shall cease to have effect; or

(*b*) subject to such conditions as may be specified in the order, shall not apply to any exclusion agreement made in relation to an arbitration award of a description so specified;

and an order under this subsection may contain such supplementary, incidental and transitional provisions as appear to the Secretary of State to be necessary or expedient.

(4) The power to make an order under subsection (2) or subsection (3) above shall be exercisable by statutory instrument which shall be subject to annulment in pursuance of a resolution of either House of Parliament.

(5) In this section 'exclusion agreement' has the same meaning as in section 3 above.

Interlocutory orders
5.—(1) If any party to a reference under an arbitration agreement falls within the time specified in the order or, if no time is so specified, within a reasonable time to comply with an order made by the arbitrator or umpire in the course of the reference, then, on the application of the arbitrator or umpire or of any party to the reference, the High Court may make an order extending the powers of the arbitrator or umpire as mentioned in subsection (2) below.

(2) In an order made by the High Court under this section, the arbitrator or umpire shall have power, to the extent and subject to any conditions specified in that order, to continue with the reference in default of appearance or of any other act by one of the parties in like manner as a judge of the High Court might continue with proceedings in that court where a party fails to comply with an order of that court or a requirement of rules of court.

(3) Section 4(5) of the Administration of Justice Act 1970 (jurisdiction

of the High Court to be exercisable by the Court of Appeal in relation to judge-arbitrators and judge-umpires) shall not apply in relation to the power of the High Court to make an order under this section, but in the case of a reference to a judge-arbitrator or judge-umpire that power shall be exercisable as in the case of any other reference to arbitration and also by the judge-arbitrator or judge-umpire himself.

(4) Anything done by a judge-arbitrator or judge-umpire in the exercise of the power conferred by subsection (3) above shall be done by him in his capacity as judge of the High Court and have effect as if done by that court.

(5) The preceding provisions of this section have effect notwithstanding anything in any agreement but do not derogate from any powers conferred on an arbitrator or umpire, whether by an arbitration agreement or otherwise.

(6) In this section 'judge-arbitrator' and 'judge-umpire' have the same meaning as in Schedule 3 to the Administration of Justice Act 1970.

Minor amendments relating to awards and appointment of arbitrators and umpires

6.—(1) In subsection (1) of section 8 of the principal Act (agreements where reference is to two arbitrators deemed to include provision that the arbitrators shall appoint an umpire immediately after their own appointment)—

(*a*) for the words 'shall appoint an umpire immediately' there shall be substituted the words 'may appoint an umpire at any time'; and
(*b*) at the end there shall be added the words 'and shall do so forthwith if they cannot agree'.

(2) For section 9 of the principal Act (agreements for reference to three arbitrators) there shall be substituted the following section:—

> **'Majority award of three arbitrators**
> 9. Unless the contrary intention is expressed in the arbitration agreement, in any case where there is a reference to three arbitrators, the award of any two of the arbitrators shall be binding.'

(3) In section 10 of the principal Act (power of court in certain cases to appoint an arbitrator or umpire) in paragraph (*c*) after the word 'are', in the first place where it occurs, there shall be inserted the words 'required or are' and the words from 'or where' to the end of the paragraph shall be omitted.

(4) At the end of section 10 of the principal Act there shall be added the following subsection:—

> '(2) In any case where—
> (*a*) an arbitration agreement provides for the appointment of an arbitrator or umpire by a person who is neither one of the

parties nor an existing arbitrator (whether the provision applies directly or in default of agreement by the parties or otherwise), and

(b) that person refuses to make the appointment or does not make it within the time specified in the agreement or, if no time is so specified, within a reasonable time,

any party to the agreement may serve the person in question with a written notice to appoint an arbitrator or umpire and, if the appointment is not made within seven clear days after the service of the notice, the High Court or a judge thereof may, on the application of the party who gave the notice, appoint an arbitrator or umpire who shall have the like powers to act in the reference and make an award as if he had been appointed in accordance with the terms of the agreement.'

Application and interpretation of certain provisions of Part I of principal Act

7.—(a) References in the following provisions of Part I of the principal Act to that Part of that Act shall have effect as if the preceding provisions of this Act were included in that Part, namely,—

(a) section 14 (interim awards);
(b) section 28 (terms as to costs of orders);
(c) section 30 (Crown to be bound);
(d) section 31 (application to statutory arbitrations); and
(e) section 32 (meaning of 'arbitration agreement').

(2) Subsections (2) and (3) of section 29 of the principal Act shall apply to determine when an arbitration is deemed to be commenced for the purposes of this Act.

(3) For the avoidance of doubt, it is hereby declared that the reference in subsection (1) of section 31 of the principal Act (statutory arbitrations) to arbitration under any other Act does not extend to arbitration under [section 64 of the County Courts Act 1984] (cases in which proceedings are to be or may be referred to arbitration) and accordingly nothing in this Act or in Part I of the principal Act applies to arbitration under the said section 92.

Short title, commencement, repeals and extent

8.—(1) This Act may be cited as the Arbitration Act 1979.

(2) This Act shall come into operation on such day as the Secretary of State may appoint by order made by statutory instrument; and such an order—

(a) may appoint different days for different provisions of this Act and for the purposes of the operation of the same provision in relation to different descriptions of arbitration agreement; and (*b*) may contain such supplementary, incidental and transitional provisions as appear to the Secretary of State to be necessary or expedient.

(3) In consequence of the preceding provisions of this Act, the following provisions are hereby repealed, namely—

(*a*) in paragraph (*c*) of section 10 of the principal Act the words from 'or where' to the end of the paragraph.
(*b*) section 21 of the principal Act;
(*c*) in paragraph 9 of Schedule 3 to the Administration of Justice Act 1970, in sub-paragraph (1) the words '21(1) and (2)' and sub-paragraph (2).

(4) This Act forms part of the law of England and Wales only.

Appendix 3

Specimen notice, letter, check list and statement

Section A: Specimen notice referring dispute to arbitration

IN THE MATTER OF THE ARBITRATION ACTS, 1950 and 1979
and
IN THE MATTER OF AN ARBITRATION

BETWEEN:

RAFFERTY (SOUTH WEST) LTD	Claimants
and	
COLDFERN BOROUGH COUNCIL	Respondents

WHEREAS on the 28th day of August 1988 the Claimants and the Respondents entered into a Contract whereby the Claimants agreed to carry out certain works namely improvements to 12 flats and 2 entrance lobbies and stairs at Clevedon Square, Coldfern for the Respondents.

AND WHEREAS the said Contract was based upon the Conditions of the Intermediate Form of Building Contract 1984 incorporating Amendments 1 to 4 inclusive.

AND WHEREAS it was provided by Article 5 of the Articles of Agreement that any dispute or difference would thereby be referred to arbitration in accordance with Clause 9 of the Conditions.

AND WHEREAS disputes and differences within the meaning of the said Clause 9 have arisen namely:

1.   The Respondents are in breach of implied and/or express terms of the Contract relating to their obligations to the Claimants to give possession of and/or access to flats, entrance lobbies and stairs as to both time and sequence.

2.   The architect has wrongfully failed to certify reimbursement to the Claimants direct loss and/or expense which they have incurred as a result of deferred possession, late instructions or details, instructions

issued in regard to postponement of work and instructions requiring variations or which are to be regarded as variations.

3.   The architect has wrongfully failed to issue instructions postponing work as and when the Respondents were unable to give access to flats, entrance lobbies and stairs in accordance with their obligations under the Contract;

4.   The architect has wrongfully failed to issue appropriate instructions relating to inconsistencies between Contract Documents and divergencies between Contract Documents and Statutory Requirements concerning access to flats, entrance lobbies and stairs;

5.   Without prejudice to the particularity of the foregoing any other disputes or differences which have arisen between us.

AND WHEREAS the said disputes and differences will be particularised in the Claimants Statement of Case yet to be served.

AND WHEREAS by Clause 9.8 of the Conditions, it is provided that the arbitration shall be conducted in accordance with the JCT Arbitration Rules current at the Base Date namely 30th July 1988.

TAKE NOTICE that in the event of the parties failing to agree on a person to act as arbitrator before 15th July 1989 that, the Claimants, will forthwith and without further notice request that the President of the Royal Institute of British Architects make the appointment of the Arbitrator as provided for in the aforesaid Article 5, clause 9.1 of the Conditions and the Appendix to the Conditions.

DATED this 1st day of July 1989

SIGNED . . . .
for and on behalf of Rafferty (South West) Ltd registered office 1 Main Street, Coldfern where service of documents will be accepted.

Section B: Specimen letter confirming appointment and setting up preliminary meeting

Dated: 31st August 1989

Gentlemen,

<u>In the matter of an arbitration between ABC Ltd and XYZ Ltd</u>

1.   I have been appointed by the President of the Royal Institute of British Architects as Arbitrator in the matter of a dispute between the parties referred to arbitration pursuant to a Notice of Arbitration dated 1st July 1989.

2.   I confirm that the arbitration is to be conducted in accordance with the JCT Arbitration Rules dated 18th July 1988 which appear to be the appropriate Rules on the assumption of a Base Date of 30th July 1988. If either party contends that some other Base Date applies could they please let me know immediately.

3.   I confirm that the notification date for the purpose of the JCT Arbitration Rules is the date of this letter namely 31st August 1989.

4.   I confirm the terms of my appointment.

(Set out here agreed terms of appointment or refer to previous correspondence where appropriate.)

5.   I propose holding a preliminary meeting at 10 O'Clock on Tuesday 18th September 1989 at the Coach House, Lower Marston, Near Bristol.

6.   At the preliminary meeting I shall expect the parties or their representatives as appropriate to address me either on their joint decision as to which of Rules 5, 6 or 7 is to apply to the conduct of the arbitration or, if no joint agreement is reached, then to let me have their views on the appropriate rule. In order to do this it is imperative that the parties or their representatives be fully conversant with the nature of the dispute or differences and that areas of agreement and disagreement are fully canvassed and identified to me. The parties should consider liaising before the preliminary meeting with a view to narrowing issues as far as possible. I shall also be asking the parties to assist me in estimating the likely length of any hearing in the event that Rule 6 applies to the conduct of the arbitration.

7.   If the Claimant wishes Rule 7 to apply, I would remind him of the requirements of Rule 4.2 which must be complied with in advance of the preliminary meeting and I look forward to receiving a copy of the written

case and statement that at the preliminary meeting he will be requesting the Respondent to agree that Rule 7 should apply.

8.   I remind the parties that the JCT Arbitration Rules contain certain very strict time-tables in connection with the delivery of statements. Failure to serve any statement in accordance with the prescribed or directed time-table under Rules 5 or 6, as applicable, can involve the parties in very serious consequences.

9.   As required by Rule 3.1 of the JCT Arbitration Rules, can each party please notify the other and me of the address for service upon them of statements, documents and notices referred to in the Rules.

10.   I enclose herewith a checklist of possible matters for consideration at the forthcoming preliminary meeting.

Yours faithfully.

Section C: Checklist of matters for consideration at preliminary meeting or as the basis of directions if preliminary meeting dispensed with

CHECKLIST

1.   If JCT Arbitration Rules have been amended since the Base Date in Appendix to Contract (or the date of Agreement in respect of the JCT Minor Works) do the parties wish to use the amended rules. If so a joint agreement in writing is required.

2.   Following discussion of the issues, identify and record principal areas of agreement and disagreement.

3.   Is there any possibility of joinder of parties?

4(a)   Is there to be an exclusion agreement under Section 3 of the Arbitration Act 1979? If so parties to agree in writing. Does either party require a reasoned award? If so party requiring it must so state in writing in accordance with Rule 11.1.

4(b)   Consider whether reasoned award should be given in any event and if so question of fees to be agreed.

5.   Selection of appropriate Rule from Rule 5, Rule 6 or Rule 7.

6.   If Rule 7 is agreed by the parties fix hearing date and give other appropriate directions to suit the case.

7.   If Rule 5 is to apply consider whether in addition to the prescribed statements there should be one further statement following any Statement of Reply.

8.   If Rule 6 is to apply consider whether any proofs of evidence whether of fact or expert opinion be appended to statements.

9.   Consider whether specific issues in the dispute can be split off to Rules 5, 6 or 7 as appropriate. If so parties to expressly consent.

10.   If Rule 5 or 6 is to apply consider whether time-table should be as prescribed by the Rules or otherwise directed?

11.   In relation to service of statements by facsimile under Rule 3.2, if documentation voluminous consider agreeing that such documents should be sent separately by first class post at the same time as the facsimile statement and that this be regarded as good service.

12.   Copies of statements to be served under the Rules to be sent to arbitrator at the same time as to the other party.

13.   If either party fails to comply with time-table other party to notify arbitrator immediately of non-service and/or late service.

14. Is arbitrator to use his expert knowledge and experience to decide the issues or is he to rely only upon expert evidence adduced.

15. Consider other directions including:

    (a) Inspection under Rule 8;

    (b) Agreement as to correspondence, plans, photographs, figures, etc;

    (c) Number of experts;

    (d) Exchange of experts reports (decision required as to whether it should be without prejudice or on an open basis and whether a joint minute of the meeting should be produced);

    (e) Date, time, place and estimated length of hearing if appropriate.

16. Liberty to apply.

17. Costs.

Author's Note

Due to the inclusion with statements of case, defence, counterclaim and reply of lists of relevant documents together with copies of them (Rule 5) or copies of the principal documents (Rule 6) the question of further discovery of documents as well as directions relating to trial bundles, and the question of sub-trials will normally be dealt with once service of the statements has taken place.

Section D: Specimen statements

1. Specimen Statement of Case under Rule 5.
2. Specimen Statement of Defence under Rule 5.
3. Specimen Statement of Case under Rule 6.
4. Specimen Statement of Defence under Rule 6.
5. Specimen Statement of Reply under Rule 6.

Notes:

1. In practice the Statements are likely to be considerably more detailed than those which follow, particularly those under Rule 5 where written submissions are used to the exclusion of any oral presentation. Constraints of space make such detail inappropriate here. However, it is hoped that the general format will be of assistance.
2. The factual content of the disputes depicted in the specimen statements are only very vaguely based upon real situations. Much has been altered or added. They are not intended to withstand detailed technical scrutiny.
3. No specimen written case under Rule 7 has been included. The nature of the Rule 7 procedure and the straightforward but highly varied situations where the Rule 7 procedure may be appropriate is such that a specimen would serve little purpose. Almost by definition therefore there can be no specimen written case.

1. Specimen statement of case under Rule 5

PROCEDURE WITHOUT A HEARING

(Dispute as to interpretation of contract documents and conditions without legal argument – JCT 80)

IN THE MATTER OF THE ARBITRATION ACTS 1950 TO 1979 AND IN THE MATTER OF AN ARBITRATION

BETWEEN:

Y. CONSTRUCTION LTD	<u>Claimants</u>
and	
Z. HEALTHCARE LTD	<u>Respondents</u>

CLAIMANTS STATEMENT OF CASE

THE PARTIES AND THE CONTRACT

1. The Claimant is main contractor and the Respondent is employer under a JCT 80 Standard Form of Building Contract with Quantities Private Edition (incorporating Amendments 1 to 6 inclusive) and dated 1st August 1988 for the construction of a private hospital.

ISSUES

2.1 Whether there has been a departure from the method of preparation of the Contract Bills under clause 2.2.2.1 of the Conditions of any error or omission such that it should be corrected under clause 2.2.2.2 and treated as if it were a variation under clause 13.2.

2.2 Whether the provision of a ring and pole system of window opening gear complies with the Specification Section of the Contract Bills.

2.3 Whether there has been a divergence between the Contract Drawings and the Contract Bills and/or a discrepancy within the Contract Bills such that an architect's instruction pursuant to clause 2.3 is required.

RELEVANT DOCUMENTS   Page references

3.1 Clause 2 and Clause 13.2 of the Conditions   1–2

3.2 Contract Bills – Preliminary Specification Section
Metalwork and Windows   3–8

3.3 SMM6 Section Q – Metalwork   9–11

Author's note:
Relevant extracts should be copied, bundled and paginated and
marked up to show the parts relied upon – see Rule 5.3. If the
relevant documents are numerous this paragraph should be
omitted and a separate list prepared and attached as an appendix
to the claim.

RELEVANT FACTS

4.1 Section 19 of the Specification within the Preliminary Section of the
Contract Bills ('Section 19') requires the Claimant to provide
aluminium windows (page 4) and provides that the windows are to
comply (page 5) with the requirements of a document called
DHSS Health Technical Memorandum Building Components
No. 55 (Windows) ('HTM 55').

4.2 HTM 55 is written in the form of guidance notes and uses such
phrases as 'consideration should be given to . . .' (page 27) and 'it
is recommended that . . .' (page 32). Nowhere does it contain
peremptory terms such as 'must' or 'shall'.

4.3 Paragraph 3.71 of HTM 55 (page 16) when referring to window
opening methods states that 'the use of poles should be avoided'.

4.4 Paragraph 2.3 of Section 19 (page 5) lists recommended window
systems describing them as 'suitable products which generally
comply with the Specification'. One of the listed systems is the
Prima System.

4.5 The Prima System uses the ring and pole method for opening
windows.

4.6 Drawing AB/123 (page 47) shows the windows as being opened by
using a vertical slider.

4.7 SMM 6 Section Q3 – Windows and doors – paragraph 2 (page 9)
provides that 'Opening gear shall be separately described . . .'.

4.8 The Contract Bills has no separate item for window opening gear.

4.9 The Claimant has provided the Prima System of windows with the
ring and pole opening method.

4.10   The architect has insisted firstly, that some form of vertical sliding gear be fitted to the windows, and secondly, that this is required by Drawing AB/123 (page 47) and further claims that

.1   there has been a permitted express departure from SMM 6;

.2   there has been no divergency between the Contract Drawings and the Contract Bills and no discrepancy within the Contract Bills.

4.11   The Claimant immediately upon discovering the same notified the architect in writing by letter dated 18th November 1988 (page 48) that there was in the Claimant's view a divergence between the Contract Drawings and Contract Bills or a discrepancy within the Contract Bills.

CLAIMANT'S CONTENTIONS

5.1   SMM 6 Section Q3 paragraph 2 (page 9) which requires a separate item for window opening gear has not been complied with. The Contract Bills have not been prepared in accordance with SMM 6. There is a departure error or omission as to the provision of window opening gear which should be corrected under clause 2.2.2.2 and treated as if it were a variation requested by an instruction of the architect under clause 13.2.

5.2   Paragraph 3.71 of HTM 55 (page 16) which provides that 'the use of poles should be avoided' is not set in obligatory language so as to be a contractual obligation. It is a mere recommendation and the provision of a ring and pole system is not a failure to comply with Section 19.

5.3   The use of the Prima System of aluminium windows is recommended by paragraph 2.3 of Section 19 (page 5) which expressly provides that this system complies with Section 19. The Claimants fully complied with the Specification in providing the Prima System. If contrary to its contention paragraph 3.71 of HTM 55 (page 16) imposes a contractual requirement to avoid the use of poles there is a clear discrepancy between two parts of the Specification which requires an architect's instruction to resolve the discrepancy.

5.4   Section 19 permits the use of ring and pole method. Contract Drawing AB/123 indicates the use of sliding vertical gear. There is clearly a divergence between the Contract Bills and the Contract Drawings so that an architect's instruction is required to resolve this divergence.

REMEDIES SOUGHT

6.   The arbitrator is asked to make declarations and to issue consequential orders and architects instructions as appropriate as follows or as may otherwise be just.

6.1 Declare that the provision of a ring and pole system of window opening gear complies with the Specification Section in the Contract Bills.

6.2 Declare that there has been a departure from the method of preparation of the Contract Bills under clause 2.2.2.1 or an omission or error therein in that there is no item relating to window opening gear and to correct the Contract Bills accordingly.

Further or alternatively

6.3 Declare that there is a divergence between the Contract Drawing AB/123 and the Contract Bills in that the former requires the use of vertical sliding gear whereas the latter permits the use of a ring and pole system and to issue an instruction to remove the divergence.

6.4 Declare that there is a discrepancy in the Contract Bills in that it both permits and prohibits a ring and pole system and issue an instruction to remove the discrepancy.

6.5 Costs.

Dated 1st February 1989.

2. Specimen statement of defence under Rule 5

PROCEDURE WITHOUT A HEARING

(Dispute as to interpretation of contract documents and conditions without legal argument – JCT 80)

IN THE MATTER OF THE ARBITRATION ACTS 1950 TO 1979 AND IN THE MATTER OF AN ARBITRATION

BETWEEN:

Y. CONSTRUCTION LIMITED	Claimants
and	
Z. HEALTHCARE LIMITED	Respondents

RESPONDENT'S STATEMENT OF DEFENCE

THE PARTIES AND THE CONTRACT

1. Paragraph 1 of the Claimants Statement of Case is agreed.

ISSUES

2. Paragraph 2 of the Claimants Statement of Case is agreed.

RELEVANT DOCUMENTS

3. Paragraph 3 of the Claimant's Statement of Case is agreed. The Respondent does not wish to refer to any additional documents but certain of the same documents are also attached to this Statement of Defence with different parts marked up upon which the Respondent relies.

RELEVANT FACTS

4. The facts as set out in the Claimant's Statement of Case are agreed.

RESPONDENT'S CONTENTIONS

5.1 While SMM 6 Section Q3 paragraph 2 (page 9) does require a separate item for window opening gear and it is accepted that there is no such separate item in the Contract Bills, nevertheless Section 19 (page 4) provides that the Claimants are to 'provide an aluminium window system complete'. A system without window opening gear would not be complete.

    Accordingly it was clear from the Contract Bills that window opening gear was required and was to be included in the tender and therefore to be within the Contract Sum from the outset. Any departure from the method of preparation set out in SMM 6 was therefore expressly covered as is permitted under clause 2.2.2.1.

Therefore the Contract Bills have been prepared in accordance with the method referred to in clause 2.2.2.1. and clause 2.2.2.2 has no application.

5.2 The Respondent now turns to which type of window opening gear was required by the Contract Documents and makes the following points:

  .1 The Contract Drawing AB/123 (page 47) clearly provides that it shall be vertical sliding gear. This cannot include a ring and pole system.

  .2 Section 19 (page 5) provides expressly that the system for the aluminium windows ' *must* comply with . . .' HTM 55. This is peremptory or obligatory in language making it a contractual requirement.

  .3 Paragraph 3.71 of HTM 55 (page 16) expressly states that 'the use of poles should be avoided'. Taken together with .2 above this is sufficient to make it clear that the use of the ring and pole system would not meet the Specification.

  .4 Paragraph 2.3 of Section 19 (page 5) lists certain recommended systems including the Prima System. However, it says that the systems listed are 'suitable products which *generally* comply with the Specification'. The use of the word 'generally' is deliberate. Many of the proprietary systems are generally acceptable but nevertheless depart from HTM 55 in specific details. The Prima System so departs in relation to the window opening gear as it uses a ring and pole system. There are a number of proprietary systems of vertical sliding gear which are fully compatible with the Prima System and one of these ought to have been included by the Respondent in its tender submission.

  .5 Having regard to points 2, 3 and 4 above, there is no divergence between the Contract Drawings and the Contract Bills and no discrepancy within the Contract Bills. Thus clause 2.3 of the Conditions has no application.

FINDINGS SOUGHT

6. The arbitrator is asked to make findings as follows:

  6.1 That the Contract Bills in relation to the window opening gear specifically provide for a method of measurement which departs from SMM 6.

6.2 That there is no divergence between the Contract Drawings and Contract Bills and no discrepancy within the Contract Bills in relation to the window opening gear.

6.3 Costs in favour of the Respondent.

Dated 12th February 1989.

LIST
(Insert here list of documents relied upon with paginated copies thereof and relevant parts relied upon marked up – Rule 5.3)

Author's note:
It might well be possible to develop legal arguments in relation to the interpretation of contract documents and/or specific conditions of contract though in a case such as this it is not likely to make a useful contribution. If legal argument is raised then the basis of this can be included within an additional paragraph of the Statement of Case and Statement of Defence together with an appendix containing appropriate extracts from statutes, cases, text books, etc., with relevant parts being marked up.

3. Specimen statement of case under Rule 6

FULL PROCEDURE WITH A HEARING
(JCT 81 WCD)

IN THE MATTER OF THE ARBITRATION ACTS 1950 TO 1979 AND IN THE MATTER OF AN ARBITRATION

BETWEEN:

PRECINCT DEVELOPMENTS PLC   <u>Claimants</u>

and

A. B. DESIGN AND BUILD LIMITED   <u>Respondents</u>

CLAIMANT'S STATEMENT OF CASE

THE PARTIES AND THE CONTRACT

1.   The Claimant is the employer and the Respondent is the contractor under a Standard Form of Building Contract with Contractor's Design 1981 Edition (incorporating Amendments 1 to 4 inclusive) dated 1st August 1988 and incorporating Employer's Requirements and Contractor's Proposals in relation to the design and construction of a shopping precinct.

ISSUES

2.   The failure in use of clay brick paviors; the reasons therefore and the legal consequences.

RELEVANT FACTS

3.1   The Employer's Requirements provides as follows:

   3.1.1   At paragraph 24.18

   'The pedestrian areas of the precinct shall be surfaced with Super Set Brick Paviors manufactured by Stubbard Brick Company Limited.'

   3.1.2   At paragraph 25.1

   'All work shall be fully protected until handed over at Practical Completion in a clean condition.'

3.2   The Respondents are well aware that the Claimants had never selected or used Stubbard's Brick Paviors in any of its previous developments and that the Claimant's reason for the inclusion of Stubbards Brick Paviors was because they were aesthetically pleasing and of a very distinctive colour and pattern. The Respondents were also aware that the Claimants desired some such distinctive feature to the pedestrian areas of all of its future shopping precinct developments as a 'hall mark' of its schemes.

3.3 The Employer's Requirements included the Stubbard's literature and detailed specification for its full range of paviors. Such literature states that the Super Set Brick Paviors were suitable for pedestrian ways.

3.4 The Contractor's Proposals provided for Stubbard Super Set Brick Paviors.

3.5 The paviors deteriorated rapidly in use and within 18 months of Practical Completion significant areas had disintegrated becoming a source of danger to pedestrians.

3.6 The deterioration took the form of indentations, cracking and splintering under the point loading of stiletto heels.

3.7 The Respondents have declined to replace these paviors at their own costs and expense.

3.8 The Claimants have had the paviors replaced with second generation Stubbard All Weather Brick Paviors at a cost which is summarised below and particularised in a Schedule attached to this Statement of Case:

	£
— removal of original paviors and replacement with new paviors	385,500.00
— tenants' disruption claims	118,750.00
— professional fees	24,000.00
TOTAL . . .	£528,250.00

CLAIMANT'S CONTENTIONS

4.1 The deterioration in the paviors is greater than could be expected from fair wear and tear.

4.2 The deterioration is due to the failure by the Respondents to properly protect the paviors in that immediately prior to Practical Completion they cleaned the paviors with a highly caustic liquid solution applied at very high temperatures causing damage to the surface of the paviors weakening it contrary to the express requirements of paragraph 25.1 of the Employer's Requirements and in breach generally by the Respondents of their contractual obligations to carry out work in a good and workmanlike manner and to provide materials of good and proper quality and of the kinds and standards described in the Employer's Requirements and the Contractor's Proposals.

4.3 Alternatively, if, which is not admitted, the paviors selected were inherently unsuitable for their intended purpose as surfacing for pedestrian ways outdoors, the Respondent had a contractual and/or tortious duty to warn the Claimants that the paviors chosen were unsuitable for their proposed use.

4.4 The Respondents failed to exercise the required contractual standard of care, namely that to be expected of a competent architect or other professional designer in the discharge of its contractual duties as well as its duty of care in tort as above.

Particulars

Failing to make proper or adequate enquiries as to the suitability of the paviors for their intended application and/or in not advising or warning the Claimants on their use outdoors.

LEGAL BASIS OF THE CLAIM

5.1 *Work and materials*

5.1.1 Clause 2.1 of the Conditions provides as follows

'The Contractor shall upon and subject to the Conditions carry out and complete the Works referred to in the Employer's Requirements, the Contractor's Proposals . . . in accordance with the aforementioned documents and for that purpose shall complete the design for the Works including the selection of any specifications for any kinds and standards of the materials and goods and workmanship to be used in the construction of the Works so far as not described or stated in the Employer's Requirements of Contractor's Proposals.'

5.1.2 Clause 8.1.1 of the Conditions provides

'All materials and goods shall . . . be of the respective kinds and standards described in the Employers Requirements . . .'

5.1.3 There were also implied terms in the contract that the Respondents would provide materials for the contract which were good of their kind and would carry out their contractual obligations using proper skill and care.

5.2 *Design*

5.2.1 Clause 2.1 of the Conditions as stated in paragraph 5.1.1 above is repeated.

5.2.2 Clause 2.5.1 provides as follows

'Insofar as the design of the Works is comprised in the Contractor's Proposals and in what the Contractor is to complete under clause 2 and in accordance with the Employer's Requirements . . . the Contractor shall have in respect of any defect or insufficiency in such design the like liability to the Employer, whether under statute or otherwise, as would an architect or, as the case may be, other appropriate professional designer holding himself out as competent to take on work for such design who, acting independently under a separate contract with the Employer, had supplied such design for or in connection with the Works to be carried out and completed by a building contractor not being the supplier of the design.'

5.2.3 Clause 2.5.4 provides as follows

'Any references to the design which the Contractor has prepared or shall prepare or issue for the Work shall include a reference to any design which the Contractor has caused or shall cause to be prepared or issued by others.'

5.2.4 There was an implied term in the contract, alternatively an independent tortious duty of care on the part of the Respondent that the Respondent would warn the Claimants of any defects in the instructions or requirements given in the Employer's Requirements.

5.3 *Legal Authorities*

There is attached as an Appendix hereto a list of relevant statutes, cases and text books together with marked up extracts upon which the Claimant relies.

REMEDIES SOUGHT

6. An award as follows or otherwise as may be just.

6.1 Damages of £528,250.00.

6.2 Costs.

Dated 1st February 1991.

SCHEDULE OF DAMAGES

(Insert list of and relevant marked up paginated extracts relied upon from statutes, cases law and text books – see Rule 3.4).

APPENDIX

(Insert list of and relevant marked up paginated extracts relied upon from statutes, cases law and test books – see Rule 3.4).

LIST

(Enumerate all documents relied upon and attach paginated bundle of principal documents (or relevant extracts) with those parts relied upon marked up – See Rule 6.3).

Author's note
The issue of unsuitability raised in paragraph 4.3 could have been omitted leaving the Respondent to raise it in the Statement of Defence with the Claimants dealing with it in the Statement of Reply. However it is assumed here that the Claimants are aware that this issue is to be raised and that it can conveniently be dealt with in this way.

4. Specimen statement of defence under Rule 6

FULL PROCEDURE WITH A HEARING
(JCT 81 WCD)

IN THE MATTER OF THE ARBITRATION ACTS 1950 TO 1979 AND IN THE MATTER OF AN ARBITRATION

BETWEEN:

PRECINCT DEVELOPMENTS PLC   <u>Claimants</u>

and

A. B. DESIGN AND BUILD LIMITED   <u>Respondents</u>

RESPONDENTS STATEMENT OF DEFENCE

THE PARTIES AND THE CONTRACT

1.   Paragraph 1 of the Claimant's Statement of Case is agreed.

ISSUES

2.   Paragraph 2 of the Claimant's Statement of Case is agreed.

RELEVANT FACTS

3.1   Paragraph 3.1 of the Claimant's Statement of Case is agreed.

3.2   As to paragraph 3.2 of the Claimant's Statement of Case the Respondents first became aware of the matters stated only after the contract was entered into.

3.3   Paragraph 3.3 of the Claimant's Statement of Case is agreed.

3.4   Paragraph 3.4 of the Claimant's Statement of Case is agreed.

3.5   Paragraph 3.5 of the Claimant's Statement of Case is agreed.

3.6   Paragraph 3.6 of the Claimant's Statement of Case is agreed so far as it goes but reference is made to the further facts referred to in paragraphs 3.9 to 3.12 inclusive.

3.7   Paragraph 3.7 of the Claimant's Statement of Case is agreed but reference is made to 3.8.1. below.

3.8   As to paragraph 3.8 of the Claimant's Statement of Case it is agreed that the paviors have been replaced in the manner stated and that the costs associated therewith have been incurred but the following additional facts are relevant

3.8.1 The Claimants did not give the Respondents a full and proper opportunity to undertake the replacement work. The Respondents offered to carry out the work upon payment to them by the Claimants of a sum of £245,000.00 without prejudice to the outcome of these proceedings.

3.8.2 The Claimants did not seek competitive tenders.

The following further facts are relevant

3.9 The Claimants who are responsible for the maintenance of the pedestrianised areas of the precinct have regularly used a highly caustic solution known as Staycleen.

3.10 The pedestrianised area is outdoors and is and has been exposed to the elements including frost action.

3.11 The Stubbard Super Set Brick Paviors were designed for outdoor use.

3.12 The paviors are not designed to and are not capable of resisting frost action.

3.13 The cleansing solution used by the Respondents was caustic free.

3.14 The second generation Stubbard All Weather Brick Paviors are specifically treated to make them resistant to frost as well as point loading of stiletto heels which renders them suitable for outdoor use.

RESPONDENT'S CONTENTIONS

4.1 The cleansing solution used which was 'Liftoff' does not contain any caustic or other deleterious substance capable of damaging the paviors.

4.2 Even if, which is denied, the cleansing solution did contain a caustic or other deleterious substance which damaged the paviors, the use by the Claimants themselves of a highly caustic cleansing solution would in any event and did cause the same damage so that the Respondents have caused no loss or damage.

4.3 The deterioration in the paviors under the point loading of stiletto heels was due to one or both of the following causes:

4.3.1 The paviors were inherently unsuitable for use in outdoor areas. When exposed to the elements the paviors are affected by frost action and quickly become incapable of resisting point loading from stiletto heels. When used in covered areas not exposed to the elements they are not so affected so that the paviors are able to withstand the point loading.

4.3.2 The use of a highly caustic cleansing solution by the Claimants which attacked the surface of the paviors so weakening it and rendering it unable to withstand the point loading.

4.4 The Claimants in selecting Stubbard Super Set Brick Paviors in the Employer's Requirements demonstrated that they were not relying upon the skill and judgment of the Respondents in the selection of a suitable surface for the pedestrian areas. The Respondents had no control over the design or selection of the pedestrian surface areas.

4.5 The Claimants are in the business of the development of retail shopping precincts and employ a professionally qualified and experienced building surveyor as its projects director. As such the Claimants were in a position to judge or alternatively to make enquiries as to the suitability of the chosen paviors and could have made appropriate enquiries of Stubbard which would have revealed that the paviors were designed for indoor use only and were incapable of resisting frost action.

4.6 Further the Respondents were under no duty to make enquiries concerning the suitability of the paviors and were under no duty to warn the Claimants against using them.

4.7 The Respondents used all reasonable care and skill to be expected from them in or about the selection of the Stubbard Super Set Brick Paviors.

4.8 In all these circumstances the Respondents are not responsible in contract or tort for the failure of the paviors.

4.9 The Respondents refer back to paragraph 3.8 hereof and claim that in any event:

4.9.1 The Claimants failed to take reasonable steps to mitigate their losses.

4.9.2 The second generation Stubbards All Weather Brick Paviors used by the Claimants are of an upgraded specification and more expensive. A betterment element of £80,000.00 should therefore be deducted from the Claimant's Claim.

LEGAL CONSIDERATIONS

5.1 The express contractual clauses of the Conditions referred to in paragraph 5 of the Claimant's Statement of Case are agreed as being accurate. It is denied that the Respondents are in breach of them.

COMMENTS

5.2 In relation to the implied term referred to in paragraph 5.1.3 of the

Claimant's Statement of Case this is agreed as an accurate statement of the law. It is denied that there is room for any such implied term in this Contract in relation to the paviors or their protection or cleaning. Alternatively if there is room for such an implied term then:

5.2.1 It is denied that the Respondents are in breach of it.

5.2.2 Alternatively, if which is denied, the Respondents are in breach of any such implied term such breach did not cause or contribute to the deterioration in the paviors and the Respondents refer to paragraph 4.2 hereof.

5.3 In relation to the implied term referred to in paragraph 5.2.4 of the Claimant's Statement of Case, it is denied that there is any such implied term in the circumstances of this case. For such an implied term to be incorporated the facts must show that the Claimants relied upon and that it was reasonable for them to rely upon the skill and judgment of the Respondents so as to place upon the Respondents the responsibility of checking that the Claimants had made a sound and suitable selection of surface for the pedestrian areas. There was no such reliance in this case and it would have been unreasonable for the Claimants to rely upon the Respondents in this regard.

5.4 The Respondents do not owe to the Claimants any independent tortious duty of care to avoid causing them economic loss.

5.5 *Legal authorities*

The Appendix to the Claimant's Statement of Case sets out certain relevant statutes and cases. The Respondents will refer to these together with others which have been listed in the Appendix to this Statement of Defence which also attaches extracts from the authorities relied upon with the relevant parts marked up.

FINDINGS SOUGHT

6.1 The dismissal of the Claimant's claims or their reduction as may be just.

6.2 Costs in favour of the Respondent.

Dated 26th February 1991.

APPENDIX

(Insert here list of additional statutes and cases relied upon together with extracts therefrom properly paginated and marked to identify those parts relied upon – see Rule 3.4).

LIST

(Enumerate all documents relied upon and attach paginated bundle of principal documents with those parts relied upon marked up – see Rule 6.3).

5. Specimen statement of reply under Rule 6

FULL PROCEDURE WITH A HEARING
(JCT 81 WCD)

IN THE MATTER OF THE ARBITRATION ACTS 1950 TO 1979 AND IN THE MATTER OF AN ARBITRATION

BETWEEN:

PRECINCT DEVELOPMENTS PLC	<u>Claimants</u>
and	
A. B. DESIGN AND BUILD LIMITED	Respondents

CLAIMANT'S STATEMENT OF REPLY

1. Reference is made to the further facts alleged by the Respondents in paragraphs 3.9 to 3.14 of the Statement of Defence and the Claimant's reply as follows:

As to 3.9

— It is admitted that a cleansing solution known as Staycleen has been used by the Claimants. It is denied that it is highly caustic or caustic to any degree at all. Further, on only three occasions has it been used and then in a heavily diluted form. Contrary to paragraph 4.3.2 of the Respondent's Statement of Defence it is denied that the use of this cleansing solution has caused or contributed to the deterioration of the surface of the paviors.

As to 3.10

— This is agreed.

As to 3.11

— It is admitted that the Stubbard literature stated expressly that the Super Set Brick Paviors were suitable for indoor use. It did not state that they were unsuitable for outdoor use and contrary to paragraph 4.3.1 of the Respondent's Statement of Defence it is denied that they were inherently unsuitable for use as a pedestrian surface outdoors.

As to 3.14

— It is denied that the second generation Stubbard All Weather Brick Paviors are specifically treated to make them frost resistant to render them suitable for use outdoors. It is admitted that they have been treated to a hardening process which gives them an enhanced aesthetic appearance and reduces the extent of discoloration in use.

Dated 9th March 1991.

Appendix 4

The JCT Arbitration Rules dated 18 July 1988

Rule 1   Arbitration Agreements

1   These Rules are the 'JCT Arbitration Rules' referred to in the Arbitration Agreements in:

·1   The Standard Form of Building Contract   Article 5 and clause 41
     1980 Edition, as amended

·2   The Standard Forms of Employer/Nominated   Clause 10 (NSC/2)
     Sub-Contractor Agreement (NSC/2 and NSC/2a)   Clause 8 (NSC/2a)
     1980 Edition, as amended

·3   The JCT Standard Forms of Nominated   Article 3 and clause 38
     Sub-Contract NSC/4 and NSC/4a, 1980 Edition,
     as amended

·4   The JCT Warranty by a Nominated Supplier (TNS/2:   Clause 4
     Schedule 3 of the JCT Standard Form of Tender by
     Nominated Supplier), as amended

·5   The Standard Form of Building Contract with   Article 5 and clause 39
     Contractor's Design 1981 Edition, as amended

·6   The Intermediate Form of Building Contract for   Article 5 and section 9
     Works of simple content 1984 Edition, as amended

·7   The Standard Form of Sub-Contract Conditions for   Article 4 and clause 35
     Sub-Contractors named under the Intermediate
     Form of Building Contract (NAM/SC) 1984 Edition, as
     amended

·8   The Standard Form of Management Contract   Article 8 and section 9
     1987 Edition, as amended

·9   The Standard Form of Works Contract (Works   Works Contract/1, Section 3
     Contract/1 and Works Contract/2) 1987 Edition for Article 3 and Works
     use with the Standard Form of Management   Contract/2 section 9
     Contract, as amended

·10 The Standard Form of Employer/Works Contractor Clause 7
     Agreement (Works Contract/1) 1987 Edition, as
     amended

·11 The Agreement for Minor Building Works   Article 4 and clause 9
     1980 Edition, as amended

Rule 2   Interpretation and provisions as to time

2·1   The party who has required a dispute to be referred to arbitration is referred to as
     'the Claimant'; the other party is referred to as 'the Respondent'. Where the Arbitrator
     has been appointed on a joint application the Arbitrator shall decide who will be the
     Claimant and who will be the Respondent.

2·2   The Claimant and Respondent are referred to as 'the parties' and this expression where the context so admits includes the Claimant and Respondent in any arbitration who have been joined in the proceedings under the relevant joinder provisions in the contract or sub-contract or other agreement referred to in Rule 1.

2·3   'Days' means calendar days but in computing any period of days referred to in these Rules all public holidays, the four days following Easter Monday, December 24, 27, 28, 29, 30 and 31 shall be excluded.

2·4   'Arbitration Agreement' means the relevant provisions of a contract, sub-contract or agreement under one of the contracts, sub-contracts or agreements referred to in Rule 1.

2·5   'Notification Date' means the date of notification by the Arbitrator to the parties of his acceptance of the appointment to proceed with the reference in accordance with the Arbitration Agreement and these Rules.

2·6   Where the context so admits 'award' includes an interim award.

2·7   No time required by these Rules, or by any direction of the Arbitrator, may be extended by agreement of the parties without the express written concurrence of the Arbitrator.

Rule 3   Service of statements, documents and notices – content of statements

3·1   Each party shall notify the other party and the Arbitrator of the address for service upon him of statements, documents or notices referred to in these Rules.

3·2   The service of any statements, documents or notices referred to in these Rules shall be

by actual delivery to the other party or

by first class post or

where a FAX number has previously been given to the sending party, by FAX (facsimile transmission) to that number.

Where service is by FAX, for record purposes the statement, document or notice served by FAX must forthwith be sent by first class post or actually delivered.

3·3   Subject to proof to the contrary service shall be deemed to have been effected for the purpose of these Rules upon actual delivery or two days, excluding Saturdays and Sundays, after the date of posting or upon the facsimile transmission having been effected.

3·4   Any statement referred to in these Rules shall:

be in writing

set out the factual and legal basis relied upon and

be served upon the other party and a copy sent to the Arbitrator.

3.5   Without prejudice to any award in respect of general damages any statement of case or of counterclaim shall so far as practicable specify the remedy which the party seeks and where a monetary sum is being sought the amount sought in respect of each and every head of claim.

Rule 4   Conduct of the arbitration – application of Rule 5, Rule 6 or Rule 7 – preliminary meeting

4·1   Not later than 21 days from the Notification Date the Arbitrator shall, unless he and the parties otherwise agree, hold a preliminary meeting with the parties at such place and on such day and at such time as the Arbitrator directs.

4·2   ·1   At the preliminary meeting, or if the Arbitrator and the parties have agreed that no preliminary meeting be held then not later than 21 days from the Notification Date, the parties shall jointly decide whether Rule 5 (procedure without hearing), Rule 6 (full procedure with hearing) or, subject to Rule 4·2·2, Rule 7 (short procedure with hearing) shall apply to the conduct of the arbitration.

       ·2   If the Claimant wishes Rule 7 to apply to the conduct of the arbitration he shall, within a reasonable time after the commencement of the arbitration and at least 7 days before a decision under Rule 4·2·1 is required, formulate his case in writing in sufficient detail to identify the matters in dispute and submit that written case to the Respondent with a copy to the Arbitrator and state that at the preliminary meeting he will request the Respondent to agree that Rule 7 shall apply to the conduct of the arbitration. A preliminary meeting shall be held and if at that meeting the parties so agree the provisions of Rule 7 shall thereafter apply and the Arbitrator shall issue any necessary directions thereunder; if at that meeting the parties do not so agree the Arbitrator shall issue a direction under Rule 4·3·1 as to whether Rule 5 or Rule 6 shall apply to the conduct of the arbitration.

4·3   ·1   If the parties have not jointly decided under Rule 4·2 which Rule shall apply to the arbitration the Arbitrator shall direct that Rule 5 shall apply unless the Arbitrator, having regard to any information supplied by, and/or any representations made by, the parties directs that Rule 6 shall apply.

       ·2   A direction under Rule 4·3·1 shall be issued within 28 days of the Notification Date or, if a preliminary meeting has been held, not later than 7 days after the date of the preliminary meeting.

4·4   Whichever of the Rules 5, 6 or 7 applies to the conduct of the arbitration all the other Rules so far as relevant and applicable shall apply.

Rule 5   Procedure without hearing

5·1   Rule 5 applies to the conduct of the arbitration where:

       ·1   the parties have so decided under Rule 4·2·1; or

       ·2   the provisions of Rule 4·3·1 have come into effect and the Arbitrator has not directed that Rule 6 shall apply.

5·2 The times for service required by Rule 5·3 shall apply unless, at a preliminary meeting, or, if no preliminary meeting has been held, then within 28 days of the Notification Date, the Arbitrator, after considering any representations made by the parties, has directed any times for service different from those required by Rule 5·3 in which case the times stated in such direction shall be substituted for the times required by Rule 5·3.

5·3 ·1 The Claimant shall, within 14 days after the date when Rule 5 becomes applicable, serve a statement of case.

·2 If the Claimant serves a statement of case within the time or times allowed by these Rules the Respondent shall, within 14 days after service of the Claimant's statement of case, serve

a statement of defence to the Claimant's statement of case; and

a statement of any counterclaim

·3 If the Respondent serves a statement of defence within the time or times allowed by these Rules the Claimant may, within 14 days after such service, serve a statement of reply to the defence.

·4 If the Respondent serves a statement of counterclaim within the time or times allowed by these Rules the Claimant shall, within 14 days after such service, serve a statement of defence to the Respondent's counterclaim.

·5 If the Claimant serves a statement of defence to the Respondent's statement of counterclaim within the time or times allowed by these Rules the Respondent may, within 14 days after such service, serve a statement of reply to the defence.

·6 The Claimant with

his statement of case and

any statement setting out a reply to the Respondent's statement of defence and

his statement of defence to any statement of counterclaim by the Respondent

and the Respondent with

his statement of defence and

any statement of counterclaim and

any statement setting out a reply to the Claimant's statement of defence to any counterclaim

shall include a list of any documents the Claimant or Respondent as the case may be considers necessary to support any part of the relevant statement and a copy of those documents identifying clearly in each document that part or parts on which reliance is or is being placed.

5·4 If a party does not serve a statement of

case, defence, reply to the defence, counterclaim, defence to the counterclaim or reply to the defence to the counterclaim within the relevant time required by Rule 5·3 or directed under Rule 5·2 the Arbitrator shall notify the parties that he proposes to proceed on the basis that the party will not be serving the same unless within 7 days of the date of service of that notification the relevant statement is served. If within 7 days of the date of service of that notification the relevant statement is not received the Arbitrator shall proceed on the basis that that party will not be serving the same. If the relevant statement is subsequently served it shall be of no effect unless the Arbitrator is satisfied that there was a good and proper reason both why an application was not made within the time required by Rule 5·7·1 and why a statement was not served within 7 days of the service of his notice given under Rule 5·4.

5·5   If the Claimant either does not serve his statement of case within the time or times allowed by these Rules or if served it is of no effect by reason of Rule 5·4 the Arbitrator shall make an award dismissing the claim and ordering the Claimant to pay the Arbitrator's fees and expenses and any costs hitherto incurred by the Respondent.

5·6   Provided that where either party has, or the parties have, previously delivered to the Arbitrator a statement or statements setting out the matter or matters in dispute including the factual and legal basis relied upon together with the information where relevant required by Rule 3·5 and a list of any documents and a copy of those documents as required by Rule 5·3·6, the Arbitrator may direct that such statement or statements shall stand in place of all or any of the statements or documents to be delivered in compliance with the requirements of Rule 5·3.

5·7   ·1   Subject to a written application by the Claimant or Respondent for an extension of the times for service required by Rule 5·3 or directed under Rule 5·2 being served upon the Arbitrator before the expiry of the relevant time for service, the Arbitrator may in his discretion extend by direction in writing to the Claimant and the Respondent the times for service required by Rule 5·3 or directed under Rule 5·2 provided he is satisfied that the reason for the application was in respect of matters which could reasonably be considered to be outside the control of the applicant.

       ·2   A copy of any written application under Rule 5·7·1 shall be served upon the other party who may, within 5 days of such service, serve written comments thereon upon the Arbitrator and serve a copy thereof upon the applicant. In exercising his discretion under Rule 5·7·1 the Arbitrator shall take such written comments into account.

5·8   Where the Arbitrator considers that any document listed in any of the statements referred to in Rule 5·3 or in any statement to which Rule 5·6 refers requires further clarification by an interview with the parties or otherwise, or that some further document is essential for him properly to decide on the matters in dispute the Arbitrator may require such clarification or further document by notice in writing to the Claimant or the Respondent as appropriate and shall serve a copy of that notice upon the party not required to provide such clarification or further document. Such clarification by an interview with the parties or otherwise shall be obtained in accordance with the directions of the Arbitrator and such further document shall be supplied to the Arbitrator with a copy of the other party by the Claimant or Respondent forthwith upon receipt of the notice in writing from the Arbitrator.

5·9 ·1 The Arbitrator shall publish his award within 28 days

    after receipt of the last of the statements and documents referred to in Rule 5·3
    or

    after the expiry of the last of the times allowed by these Rules for their service

whichever is the earlier.

·2 The Arbitrator may decide to publish his award later than the expiry of the aforementioned 28 days period and if so he shall, prior to the expiry thereof, immediately notify the parties in writing when his award will be published.

Rule 6 Full procedure with hearing

6·1 Rule 6 applies to the conduct of the arbitration where:

·1 the parties have so decided under Rule 4·2·1; or

·2 the provisions of Rule 4·3·1 have come into effect and the Arbitrator has directed that Rule 6 shall apply.

6·2 Rule 6·3 shall apply except to the extent that the Arbitrator otherwise directs or, subject to Rule 2·7, the parties otherwise agree.

6·3 ·1 The Claimant shall, within 28 days after the date when Rule 6 becomes applicable, serve a statement of case.

·2 If the Claimant serves a statement of case within the time or times allowed by these Rules the Respondent shall, within 28 days after service of the Claimant's statement of case, serve

    a statement of defence to the Claimant's statement of case; and

    a statement of any counterclaim.

·3 If the Respondent serves a statement of defence within the time or times allowed by these Rules the Claimant may, within 14 days after such service, serve a statement of reply to the defence.

·4 If the Respondent serves a statement of counterclaim within the time or times allowed by these Rules the Claimant shall, within 28 days after such service, serve a statement of defence to the Respondent's counterclaim.

·5 If the Claimant serves a statement of defence to the Respondent's statement of counterclaim within the time or times allowed by these Rules the Respondent may, within 14 days after such service, serve a statement of reply to the defence.

·6   The Claimant with

> his statement of case and

> any statement setting out a reply to the Respondent's statement of defence and

> his statement of defence to any statement of counterclaim by the Respondent

and the Respondent with

> his statement of defence and

> any statement of counterclaim and

> any statement setting out a reply to the Claimant's statement of defence to any counterclaim

shall include a list of any documents the Claimant or Respondent as the case may be considers necessary to support any part of the relevant statement and a copy of the principal documents on which reliance will be placed identifying clearly in each document the relevant part or parts on which reliance will be placed.

6·4   If a party does not serve a statement of

case, defence, reply to the defence, counterclaim, defence to the counterclaim or reply to the defence to the counterclaim

within the relevant time required by Rule 6·3 or directed or agreed under Rule 6·2 the Arbitrator shall notify the parties that he proposes to proceed on the basis that the party will not be serving the same unless within 7 days of the date of service of that notification the relevant statement is served. If within 7 days of the date of service of that notification the relevant statement is not received the Arbitrator shall proceed on the basis that the party will not be serving the same. If the relevant statement is subsequently served it shall be of no effect unless the Arbitrator is satisfied that there was a good and proper reason both why an application was not made within the time required by Rule 6·7·1 and why a statement was not served within 7 days of his notice given under Rule 6·4.

6·5   If the Claimant either does not serve his statement of case within the time or times allowed by these Rules or if served it is of no effect by reason of Rule 6·4 the Arbitrator shall make an award dismissing the claim and ordering the Claimant to pay the Arbitrator's fees and expenses and any costs hitherto incurred by the Respondent.

6·6   Provided that where either party has, or the parties have, previously delivered to the Arbitrator a statement or statements setting out the matter or matters in dispute including the factual and legal basis relied upon together with the information where relevant required by Rule 3·5 and a list of any documents and a copy of the principal documents as required by Rule 6·3·6, the Arbitrator may direct that such statement or statements shall stand in place of all or any of the statements or documents to be delivered in compliance with Rule 6·3.

6·7   ·1   Subject to a written application by the Claimant or Respondent for an extension of the times for service required by Rule 6·3 or directed or agreed under Rule 6·2 being served upon the Arbitrator before the expiry of the relevant time for service, the Arbitrator may in his discretion extend by direction in writing to the Claimant and the Respondent the times for service required by Rule 6·3 or directed or agreed under Rule 6·2.

·2 A copy of any written application under Rule 6·7·1 shall be served upon the other party who may, within 5 days of such service, serve written comments thereon upon the Arbitrator and serve a copy thereof upon the applicant. In exercising his discretion under Rule 6·7·1 the Arbitrator shall take such written comments into account.

6·8 The Arbitrator shall, after receipt of the last of the statements and documents referred to in Rule 6·3 or after the expiry of the last of the times allowed by these Rules for their service, whichever is the earlier, after consultation with the parties, notify the parties in writing of the date(s) when and the place where the oral hearing will be held. The Arbitrator shall immediately notify the parties in writing of any change in such date(s) or place.

6·9 ·1 The Arbitrator shall publish his award within 28 days of the close of the hearing.

·2 The Arbitrator may decide to publish his award later than the expiry of the aforementioned 28 day period and if so he shall, prior to the expiry thereof, immediately notify the parties in writing when his award will be published.

Rule 7 Short procedure with hearing

7·1 ·1 Rule 7 applies to the conduct of the arbitration where the parties have so decided under Rule 4·2·2.

·2 Each party shall bear his own costs unless for special reasons the Arbitrator at his discretion otherwise directs.

7·2 Within 21 days of the date when Rule 7 has become applicable the hearing shall be held at such place and on such day and at such time as the Arbitrator shall direct. No evidence except the documents referred to in Rule 7·3 may be adduced at the hearing except as the Arbitrator may otherwise direct or allow.

7·3 ·1 Not later than 7 days before the hearing documents necessary to support the oral submissions and the relevant part or parts thereof shall be identified to the other party and a copy of any such document not in the possession of the other party shall be served upon that party.

·2 A copy of the documents referred to in Rule 7·3·1 shall be served upon the Arbitrator 7 days before the hearing and shall be available at the hearing.

7·4 The Arbitrator may direct that such procedures shall be followed at the hearing and such documents made available as he considers necessary for the just and expeditious determination of the dispute.

7·5 At the end of the hearing the Arbitrator shall

either thereupon make his award and if made orally shall forthwith confirm his award in writing

or publish his award within 7 days of the hearing.

The Arbitrator may decide to publish his award later than the expiry of the aforementioned 7 day period and if so, he shall, prior to the expiry thereof, immediately notify the parties in writing when his award will be published.

Rule 8   Inspection by Arbitrator

8·1   The Arbitrator may inspect any relevant work, goods or materials whether on the site or elsewhere. Such inspection shall not be treated as a hearing of the dispute.

8·2   Where under Rule 8·1 the Arbitrator has decided that he will inspect:

where Rule 5 applies, as soon as the parties have served all their written statements or the last of the times for such service allowed by these Rules has expired the Arbitrator shall fix a date not more than 10 days in advance for his inspection and shall inform the parties of the date and time selected;

where Rule 6 or Rule 7 applies, the Arbitrator shall fix a date for his inspection and shall inform the parties of the date and time selected.

8·3   ·1   The Arbitrator may require the Claimant or the Respondent, or a person appointed on behalf of either of them, to attend the inspection solely for the purpose of identifying relevant work, goods or materials.

·2   No other person may attend the Arbitrator's inspection unless the Arbitrator shall otherwise direct.

Rule 9   Arbitrator's fees and expenses – costs

9·1   From the Notification Date the parties shall be jointly and severally liable to the Arbitrator for the payment of his fees and expenses.

9·2   In an arbitration which continues for more than 3 months after the Notification Date the Arbitrator shall be entitled to render fee notes at no less than 3-monthly intervals and the same shall be payable 14 days after delivery.

9·3   The Arbitrator shall, unless the parties inform him that they have otherwise agreed, include in his award his decision on the liability of the parties as between themselves for the payment of his fees and expenses and, subject to Rule 7·1·2, on the payment by one party of any costs of the other party.

9·4   The Claimant shall, unless the Respondent has previously done so, take up an award of the Arbitrator and pay his fees and expenses (or any balance thereof if Rule 9·2 has applied) within 10 days of the notification given by the Arbitrator to the parties of publication of the award as provided in Rule 11·3.

Rule 10   Payment to trustee-stakeholder

10·1   If the Arbitrator publishes an award in favour of the Claimant before he has published his award on all matters in a counterclaim by the Respondent, the Arbitrator upon application by the Claimant or the Respondent and after considering any representations by the parties may direct that the whole or a part of the amount so awarded shall be deposited by the Respondent with a deposit-taking bank to hold as a trustee-stakeholder (as described in Rule 10·3) pending a direction of the Arbitrator under Rule 10·2·1 or of the parties under Rule 10·2·2 or of the court under Rule 10·2·3.

10·2 The trustee-stakeholder shall hold any amount deposited as a result of a direction of the Arbitrator under Rule 10·1 in trust for the parties until such time as either

·1 the Arbitrator shall direct the trustee-stakeholder (whether as a result of his award or as a result of an agreement between the parties reported to the Arbitrator or otherwise) to whom the amount deposited, including any interest accrued thereon, should be paid by the trustee-stakeholder; or

·2 if the Arbitrator is deceased or otherwise unable to issue any direction to the trustee-stakeholder under Rule 10·2·1 and the Arbitrator has not been replaced, the parties in a joint letter signed by or on behalf of each of them direct the trustee-stakeholder to whom the amount deposited, including any interest accrued thereon, should be paid by the trustee-stakeholder; or

·3 a court of competent jurisdiction gives directions.

10·3 An amount so deposited may, notwithstanding the trust imposed, be held by the trustee-stakeholder as an ordinary bank deposit to the credit of the bank as a trustee-stakeholder in respect of the party making the deposit pursuant to a direction of the Arbitrator under Rule 10·1 and in respect of such deposit the trustee-stakeholder shall pay such usual interest which shall accrue to and form part of the deposit subject to the right of the trustee-stakeholder to deduct its reasonable and proper charges and, if deductible, any tax in respect of such interest from the amount deposited.

Rule 11 The award

11·1 The Arbitrator shall only give reasons for his award where and to the extent required by either party by notice in writing to the Arbitrator with a copy to the other party.

11·2 ·1 The Arbitrator may from time to time publish an interim award.

·2 If in any interim award the parties are directed to seek agreement on an amount or amounts due but such agreement is not reached by the parties within 28 days of receipt of that award (or within such other lesser or greater period as the Arbitrator may direct) the Arbitrator shall, on the basis of such further appropriate evidence or submissions as he may require, publish a further award on the amount due in respect of any liability or liabilities set out in the interim award.

11·3 On publishing an award the Arbitrator shall simultaneously send to the parties by first class post, a notification that his award is published and of the amount of his fees and expenses (or any balance thereof if Rule 9·2 has applied).

11·4 An Arbitrator's award can be taken up by either party on payment to the Arbitrator of his fees and expenses. The Arbitrator shall forthwith deliver the original award to the party who paid his fees and expenses and shall simultaneously send a certified copy of the award to the other party.

11·5 If, before an award is published, the parties agree on a settlement of the dispute the parties shall so notify the Arbitrator. The Arbitrator shall issue an order for the termination of the arbitration or, if requested by both parties and accepted by the Arbitrator, record the settlement in the form of a consent award. The Arbitrator's fees and expenses shall be paid upon notification that such order or consent award is ready for taking up and on payment thereof the Arbitrator shall be discharged and the reference to arbitration concluded.

Rule 12 Powers of Arbitrator

12·1   In addition to any other powers conferred by law, the Arbitrator shall have the following powers:

·1   after consultation with the parties to take legal or technical advice on any matter arising out of or in connection with the arbitration;

·2   to give directions for protecting, storing, securing or disposing of property the subject of the dispute, at the expense of the parties or of either of them;

·3   to order that the Claimant or Counter-Claimant give security for the costs of the arbitration or any part thereof, and/or for the fees and expenses of the Arbitrator, in such form and of such amount as the Arbitrator may determine;

·4   to proceed in the absence of a party or his representative provided that reasonable notice of the Arbitrator's intention to proceed has been given to that party in accordance with the provisions of these Rules, including if there is to be a hearing, notice of the date and place thereof;

·5   at his discretion to direct that the costs, if not agreed, shall be taxed by the Arbitrator;

·6   to direct the giving of evidence by affidavit;

·7   to order any party to produce to the Arbitrator, and to the other party for inspection, and to supply copies of, any documents or classes of documents in the possession power or custody of the party which the Arbitrator determines to be relevant.

12·2   Subject to the Arbitration Acts 1950 to 1979 any non-compliance by the Arbitrator with these Rules, including those relating to time, shall not of itself affect the validity of an award.

12·3   If during the arbitration it appears to the Arbitrator to be necessary for the just and expeditious determination of the dispute that a Rule for the conduct of the arbitration other than that previously applicable shall apply, the Arbitrator, after considering any representations made by the parties, may so direct and shall give such further directions as he may deem appropriate.

Table of Cases

Table of Statutes

Index